YOUR RIGHTS 1993-94

A guide to money benefits
for older people

SALLY WEST

BOOKS

Published by Age Concern England
1268 London Road
London SW16 4ER
© 1993 Age Concern England
Twenty-first Edition

This edition prepared by Sally West
Editorial   Caroline Hartnell
Evelyn McEwen and David Moncrieff
Design   Eugenie Dodd
Production   Marion Peat
Printed by Grosvenor Press Limited, Portsmouth

A catalogue record for this book is available from
the British Library.

ISBN 0–86242–131–4

Age Concern would like to thank the DSS for their comments
on the text. The author also acknowledges contributions from
colleagues in the Information and Policy Department.

CONTENTS

INTRODUCTION

This book provides information about the main financial benefits available for older people. Most of the social security rates given apply from the week beginning 12 April 1993.

Your Rights is divided into five parts and there is an index at the back. The first two sections give details about pensions and financial help for those on low incomes, including help with the new Council Tax. The third section covers benefits for disabled people and their carers, while the fourth part gives information about other types of financial help including the new system of help towards residential and nursing home care.

Many of the subjects covered in *Your Rights* can be complicated, and the book aims to explain them as simply as possible. However, it cannot cover all situations and circumstances. If you need more information, the fifth section gives details about relevant Department of Social Security leaflets, factsheets prepared by Age Concern England and other sources of local and national help.

Please note that although some older people have young families, benefits for children are not covered in this book.

Where you live

All the information covered in *Your Rights* applies to people living in England and Wales. The information on benefits and other sources of help also applies to Scotland except for the sections on 'Legal Aid' and 'Help with repairs and improvements'.

Although there are separate social security systems in the Isle of Man and Northern Ireland, the social security benefits available are generally the same.

The national Age Concern organisations in Scotland and Northern Ireland produce their own editions of *Your Rights* which highlight any differences between the systems. For further information or advice relating to older people living in these countries contact Age Concern Scotland or Age Concern Northern Ireland – the addresses are on page 127.

For more information on pensions and benefits for people living abroad either permanently or temporarily, you should contact your local social security office (if you are currently in this country) or the Overseas Branch of the DSS (address on p 122). They produce a series of leaflets covering social security arrangements with countries outside the United Kingdom including Jersey, Guernsey and the European Community countries.

Keeping up to date

This book is based on information available in March 1993 and should apply until the beginning of April 1994. If you would like to be kept up to date with any major changes during the year, please fill in the form on page 129.

A new edition of *Your Rights* will be available in April 1994 – please let us know if you have any comments or suggestions.

Pensions, Widow's Benefits and Retirement

This part of Your Rights *contains information about State Retirement Pensions. There is also a section on early retirement, which describes the benefits available to people who leave work before State Pension age, and another which looks at the effect on State benefits if you choose to work after pension age. In addition there are details about widow's benefits; the Christmas Bonus (paid to people receiving a State Pension or certain other benefits); the procedure for appealing against a social security decision; and occupational and personal pensions.*

RETIREMENT PENSIONS (TAXABLE)

To qualify for the State Retirement Pension you must have reached pension age (60 for women, 65 for men) and fulfil the National Insurance (NI) contribution conditions.

Your pension may consist of a Basic Pension plus an Additional Pension (based on contributions after April 1978) and a Graduated Pension (based on contributions between April 1961 and April 1975). You will receive an extra 25p when you reach the age of 80. You may also receive extra pension if you defer drawing your pension. These different parts of the pension are explained below.

Whether you are entitled to a State Pension or not, you may be able to claim other benefits such as Income Support, Housing Benefit and Council Tax Benefit, which depend on your income and savings.

See social security guide NP 46 about Retirement Pensions.

Changes to pension ages

The Government intends to introduce equal pension ages for men and women and it is expected that proposals will be announced during 1993. However, it is likely to be some time before any changes are introduced and any moves that would increase pension age for women will be phased in over a number of years.

BASIC PENSION (TAXABLE)

The Basic Pension is paid at the same rate to everyone who has fulfilled the contribution conditions.

The full weekly rates are shown below:

Single person	£56.10
Wife on husband's contributions	£33.70
Married couple on husband's contributions	£89.80
Married couple (if both paid full contributions)	£112.20

Who qualifies?

You will receive the full basic rate of pension if you have paid, or been credited with, NI contributions at the full rate for most of the years of your working life. If you have not paid enough, you may get a reduced pension or you may not get a pension at all (see 'Your contributions', pp 14–16).

Normally you need to have satisfied the contribution conditions in your own right; but married women, divorcees or widowed people may be able to claim a pension on their spouse's or ex-spouse's contributions, as explained in the following pages.

Pensions for married women

If you are a married woman and you have paid full contributions for all of your working life, you should be entitled to the Basic Pension of £56.10 a week when you become 60. If you have paid full contributions for only part of your working life, you may be entitled to a reduced pension. However, any years when you were paying the married woman's reduced contributions will not count towards a pension.

If you are 60 or over but have not paid enough contributions for a pension in your own right, you cannot get any Basic Pension until your husband draws his. When your husband draws his pension, you should claim the married woman's pension, which will be £33.70 a week if your husband has a full contribution record.

When you reach 60, if the pension on your own contributions is less than £33.70 a week, it will be made up to a maximum of £33.70 a week when your husband draws his pension. However, if your own pension is more than £33.70 a week, you cannot get any extra pension based on your husband's contributions.

Married women who worked in the 1940s

If you worked before the present National Insurance scheme started in 1948, perhaps during the war years, you may have been paying contributions which could count towards a pension now. The rules are complicated but sometimes women find that even if they have not worked for many years, the contributions they made earlier on can help them qualify for a partial pension. However, if you are already receiving a pension or another benefit, for example a pension based on your husband's contributions or a Widow's Pension, you may not be entitled to anything more.

Example

Catherine worked from 1946 until 1956 when she got married. When she became 60 she could not draw a pension on her husband's contributions because he was only 63. However, she was entitled to a small pension based on the contributions she had paid.

If you think you might be entitled to a pension, contact your local Benefits Agency (social security) office with details of when you paid contributions, your past employment, your maiden name and, if possible, your NI number.

Increases for dependants

Dependent wives

If you are under 60 when your husband draws his pension (at 65 or more) he may be able to claim for you as a dependant, and his pension will be increased by a maximum of £33.70 a week. However, if you receive a State benefit he may not be able to get this increase. It may also be affected by any earnings you have.

If you live with your husband he will not be able to receive the increase if you are working and earn more than £44.65 a week (after certain expenses connected with work have been deducted). Any occupational or personal pension you receive will be counted as earnings. (However, if you were refused an increase for a dependant because your spouse had an occupational pension at any time between 11 March 1988 and 5 December 1992 contact Age Concern England as you could benefit from a Court of Appeal decision made in December 1992.) If you do not live with your husband he will not be able to receive this increase if you earn more than £33.70 a week.

If you live with your husband and you are working and your husband retired before 16 September 1985 and he has been receiving an increase in his pension for you since then, you can earn up to £45.09 a week before this affects his increase.

Dependent husbands

If you are a married man and your wife is receiving a State Pension, she may be able to get an increase for you of up to £33.70, provided you are not earning more than £44.65 a week (£33.70 if you do not live with your wife). However, she can only get this increase if she was receiving an addition for you with Unemployment, Sickness or Invalidity Benefit immediately before she started drawing the State Pension. Your wife will not receive any increase if you have a State Pension or certain other benefits of £33.70 or more.

Pensions for divorced and separated people

Divorced people

If you are divorced but do not qualify for a full pension based on your own contributions, you may be able to use your former spouse's contribution record to increase the amount of Basic Pension you receive to a maximum of the single person's pension of £56.10 a week. Before 6 April 1979 this only applied to women who divorced before reaching pension age (60). You are not entitled to your former spouse's Graduated or Additional Pension.

You can substitute your former spouse's contribution record for your own from the start of your working life up until your divorce or just for the period of your marriage.

If you get divorced before pension age, you may need to pay further contributions after your divorce to qualify for a Basic Pension.

If you get divorced after pension age and are receiving the married woman's pension, you may be able to use the rules outlined above to get a full pension.

People who remarry

If you remarry before pension age, you cannot claim a pension on your first husband's or wife's contributions. However, if you remarry after pension age you will not lose a pension based on your previous spouse's contributions.

See social security leaflet NI 95.

Separated women

If you are separated and do not qualify for a pension on your own contributions when you reach 60, you may be able to claim the married woman's pension of up to £33.70 a week when your husband claims his.

Retirement Pensions for widows and widowers

Widows

If you were under 60 when your husband died and you have not remarried, you can draw the State Pension based on his contributions and/or your own, once you reach pension age.

If you were 60 or over when your husband died, and not receiving the full Basic Pension, then you may be able to use his contribution record to bring your Basic Pension up to a maximum of £56.10.

You will receive his Additional Pension plus your own up to the level of the maximum Additional Pension for a single person. This will be adjusted to take into account any time you and/or your husband were 'contracted out' of the State Additional Pension scheme, as explained on pages 22–23. You will also receive half of his Graduated Pension as well as any based on your own contributions.

Once you are drawing the State Pension at age 60 or over, you can remarry or live with a man as his wife without losing a pension based on your previous husband's contributions.

Widows should also see pages 31–32 on the Widow's Payment and Widow's Pension.

Widowers

If you were widowed on or after 6 April 1979 and do not have enough contributions of your own, you may be entitled to a Retirement Pension based on your wife's contributions provided you were both over pension age when she died. You may also inherit half your wife's Graduated Pension and add her Additional Pension to your own up to the maximum Additional Pension for a single person. If you do not fulfil the above conditions, perhaps because you were widowed before age 65, once you reach pension age you may be able to substitute your wife's contribution record for your own in order to increase your Basic Pension up to a maximum of £56.10 a week.

Your contributions

You will get the full Basic Pension if you have paid, or been credited with, NI contributions for most of your working life. If you have not paid enough contributions, your pension may be reduced, or you may not get one at all.

Since April 1975 employed people have paid contributions as a percentage of earnings, and these are collected with income tax.

Self-employed people pay flat-rate contributions each week which count towards the Basic Pension. If your taxable income is over a certain amount, extra contributions will be collected with your income tax.

If you paid the married woman's or widow's reduced rate contributions, these do not count towards a pension in your own right.

Contributions made abroad may help you qualify for the Basic Pension provided the country where you worked has a reciprocal agreement with the UK (contact the DSS, Overseas Branch, Newcastle Upon Tyne NE98 1YX).

Both men and women aged 80 or over who have not paid enough contributions for a Basic Pension might qualify for the non-contributory pension described on page 24.

You can check whether you have paid enough contributions to get a full pension by completing form BR 19, obtainable from your local Benefits Agency (social security) office. Whether you will get a full pension depends on your 'working life' and 'qualifying years', and whether your contribution record has been protected by 'credits' and/or 'Home Responsibilities Protection'. These terms are explained below.

Working life

Your 'working life' is the number of tax years (ie 6 April to 5 April) during which you are expected to pay, or be credited with, NI contributions. This normally starts in the tax year when you were 16 and ends with the last full tax year before your 60th (women) or 65th (men) birthday.

However, if you were over 16 when the National Insurance scheme started in 1948 and you were insured for pension purposes, your working life is counted from April 1936 or from the beginning of the tax year in which you last entered insurance between 1936 and 1948 (whichever date is later). If you were not 'in insurance' in July 1948, your working life will be counted from April 1948.

Example
Joan started work in July 1940 when she was 18. She worked until she got married in 1950. As she was over 16 in 1948, her 'working life' started in April 1940 and ended with the last full tax year before she reached 60.

Credits

If you are under pension age (60 for women, 65 for men) you may receive a credit in place of an NI contribution for each week you are signing on as unemployed and seeking work; or you are unable to work because you are sick or disabled or because you are receiving Invalid Care Allowance. Since April 1983, men aged 60–64 who are not paying contributions will normally receive credits automatically even if they are not ill or signing on as unemployed. However, men cannot get these automatic credits for any tax year during which they are abroad for more than six months.

Qualifying years

A 'qualifying year' is a tax year in which you have paid (or been credited with) enough contributions to go towards a pension.

Since 1978 a 'qualifying year' has been one in which contributions are paid on earnings which are the same as, or more than, 52 times the weekly lower earnings limit. (Between April 1975 and April 1978 the qualifying earnings were 50 times the lower earnings limit.)

The lower earnings limit is the level at which you start to pay NI contributions on all of your earnings. This tax year, 1993–94, the lower earnings limit is £56 a week. If you earn less than this, you do not pay contributions towards a pension.

Before 1975 working people paid contributions by weekly stamp. To work out your qualifying years before 1975, all your stamps (paid and credited) are added up and divided by 50, rounding up any that are left over – but you cannot have more qualifying years worked out in this way than the number of years in your working life up to April 1975.

See social security leaflets N1 196 (on contribution rates), NP 28 (NI for employees), NP 18 (NI for self-employed people).

Late and voluntary contributions

If there are periods when you will not be paying contributions, perhaps because you will be abroad, you may want to consider paying voluntary contributions to protect your pension record. If there are gaps in your contribution record, it is sometimes possible to pay late contributions. However, there are time limits for paying these voluntary contributions. Ask at your Benefits Agency (social security) office if you need advice.

See social security leaflets NI 42 (on voluntary contributions) and NI 48 (on late contributions).

Calculating your pension

To be entitled to a full pension, about nine out of every ten years in your working life have to be qualifying years, as shown below.

Length of working life	Number of qualifying years needed for a full pension
21–30 years	working life minus 3
31–40 years	working life minus 4
41 years or more	working life minus 5

If you are not entitled to the full Basic Pension, you may get a reduced one provided you have at least a quarter of the qualifying years you need for a full pension.

Example
Christine was born on 10 August 1934 and was 16 in 1950. Her working life runs from 6 April 1950 to 5 April 1994, a total of 44 years. To receive a full Basic Pension, she needs 39 or more qualifying years. If she has only worked and paid contributions for 20 years of her working life, she will receive about half the Basic Pension.

Home Responsibilities Protection

Home Responsibilities Protection (HRP) started in 1978 to protect the contribution record of people who cannot work regularly because they have to stay at home to look after a sick or disabled person or children.

You cannot get HRP for the years when you were looking after someone before April 1978. A married woman or widow cannot get HRP for any tax year in which she, if she was working, would only be due to pay reduced rate NI contributions.

You are entitled to HRP if you meet any of the following conditions, or a combination of them, for a whole tax year (but note the rules changed in 1988 for the third condition):

- you get Child Benefit for a child under 16;
- you get Income Support without having to sign on as unemployed because you are looking after someone;
- for at least 35 hours a week you look after someone who receives, for a minimum of 48 weeks in the year, Attendance Allowance, the middle or higher rate of the care component of Disability Living Allowance, or Constant Attendance Allowance.

For tax years before 6 April 1988, the allowance had to have been paid for 52 weeks. (If you get Invalid Care Allowance, you will normally be getting credits towards your pension so you will not need HRP, although you cannot get credits if you retained the right to pay the married woman's reduced rate contributions).

How to work it out

HRP makes it easier for you to qualify for a Basic Pension. Each year of 'home responsibility' will be taken away from the number of qualifying years you need to get a full pension. However, HRP cannot normally be used to reduce the number of qualifying years to below 20.

Example

Mrs Smith started work at 16 and paid full contributions for 30 years until 1978 when she gave up work to look after her mother. She was still caring for her mother when she became 60 in 1992 so her pension is worked out in the following way.

Working life	44 years
Number of qualifying years needed for a full pension	39 years
Number of years of HRP	14 years
Number of qualifying years needed for a full pension after taking away years of HRP	25 years

Because of HRP, Mrs Smith receives a full pension, as the number of qualifying years she needs is reduced to 25.

When to claim

HRP will be given automatically if you qualify under the first two conditions described above (because you get Child Benefit or Income Support). You do not have to claim.

You must claim HRP if you are looking after someone who is getting one of the allowances mentioned above, or if you have looked after someone under one condition for part of the tax year, and under another for the rest of the year. Ask for claim form CF 411.

How to claim your pension

About four months before you reach pension age you should be sent a claim form. If you have not received one three months before your birthday, write to the local Benefits Agency (social security) office. Fill in the claim form as soon as you receive it. A married woman claiming a pension on her husband's contributions will need to fill in a separate form.

You may decide not to draw your pension at 60 (women) or 65 (men) in order to gain extra pension, in which case, when you wish to start claiming the pension, you should contact your local office well in advance. Deferring your pension is explained on page 26.

Once you reach the age of 65 (women) or 70 (men), you should claim your pension as you will gain no further increases.

If you make a late claim for your pension, it can be backdated for up to one year.

How your pension is paid

There are two ways to have your pension paid. You may choose to have it paid by weekly order book which you cash at a post office. Pensions are then paid one week in advance. If you cannot get to a post office, someone else can cash your pension for you. The pension book explains how this is done.

If you prefer to have your pension paid into a bank, Girobank, building society account, or investment account with the National Savings Bank, you can have it paid directly by 'Direct Credit Transfer'; the money will then be paid in arrears and you can choose to receive it either four-weekly or quarterly.

Pay-day for anyone who started to draw their pension before 28 September 1984 is normally Thursday. For people who retired after that date, pay-day is usually Monday, although if your spouse is already receiving a pension on Thursday, you can choose to have yours on the same day. You cannot receive any pension for days of retirement before your first pay-day.

Most pensions of £2 a week or less (£1 a week for awards of pension prior to July 1987) are paid once a year, in December, in arrears. If you requested payment by Direct Credit Transfer, you will be paid by that method; if you requested payment by order book, you will be paid by crossed payable order.

See social security leaflet NI 105 (payments into bank or building society accounts).

Going abroad or living there

If you receive your pension by weekly order book and are going abroad for less than three months, you can cash all your pension orders when you come home. However, a pension order cannot be cashed more than three months after the date printed on it. If you are going abroad for more than three months, tell your local Benefits Agency (social security) office well in advance so that your pension can be paid into a bank or other account while you are away. Alternatively you may arrange for your pension to accrue and be paid in one lump sum on your return.

If you do not receive your pension by weekly order book, you do not need to tell your local office unless you are staying abroad for more than six months. You can, if you wish, arrange to receive your pension in the country where you are staying. If you remain abroad, the annual pension increase will only be paid in a European Community country or in a country with which the UK has special arrangements.

Contact your local Benefits Agency (social security) office or the DSS, Overseas Branch, Newcastle Upon Tyne NE98 1YX.

Going into hospital

If you go into hospital, you will receive your full pension for up to six weeks. After that the pension is usually reduced by £11.20 a week if you have a dependant and by £22.40 a week if you do not have a dependant. (If you are married and your husband or wife is at home then he or she will be considered as your 'dependant'.)

After one year, if you are single, you will only receive £11.20 a week. If you have a dependant, your pension will be reduced by a further £11.20 a week. You will normally be paid £11.20 of the pension and, if you agree, the rest will be paid to your dependant.

See social security leaflet NI 9.

Is your pension the wrong amount?

If you think you have been awarded the wrong amount of pension, or disagree with another decision to do with your pension, you can either ask for the decision to be reviewed or you can appeal against it. Further details about reviews and appeals are given on pages 33–34.

ADDITIONAL PENSION (TAXABLE)

The Additional Pension, paid under the State Earnings-Related Pension Scheme (SERPS), started on 6 April 1978 and is based on earnings on which you have paid contributions since then. You may qualify for an Additional Pension even if you are not entitled to the Basic Pension. There are going to be changes to the scheme but these will not affect anyone reaching State Pension age before 6 April 1999. Only the current rules are described here. Employees will be paying into SERPS unless they have 'contracted out' of the scheme, as explained below.

The Additional Pension is related to weekly earnings between certain levels known as the 'lower and upper earnings limits'. For 1993–94, the weekly limits are £56 and £420 respectively. Earnings from past years are revalued in line with increases in average earnings. Your total revalued earnings are divided by 80 to give the yearly amount of Additional Pension.

You can ask the local Benefits Agency (social security) office how to get a statement of your present Additional Pension and an estimate of what you can expect when you retire.

Contracting out of SERPS

Some occupational pension schemes are 'contracted out' of SERPS. This means the pension scheme will provide an occupational pension in place of the Additional Pension. If you are in a contracted-out occupational pension scheme, you will pay lower NI contributions. If you are not in such a scheme, you can choose to contract out of SERPS and join an approved personal pension scheme instead. If your occupational pension scheme is not contracted out, you will receive a full State Additional Pension as well as your occupational pension.

Contracted-out occupational pension schemes and appropriate personal pension schemes have to satisfy certain conditions and receive a certificate of approval from the Occupational Pensions Board.

There are two types of contracted-out occupational pension scheme: salary-related schemes and money-purchase schemes. A contracted-out salary-related (COSR) scheme will provide a pension related to your earnings. The minimum amount of pension you will receive is called the Guaranteed Minimum Pension (GMP), which is broadly equivalent to the State Additional Pension you would have received.

A contracted-out money-purchase (COMP) occupational scheme or an approved personal pension scheme gives a pension based on the value of the fund an individual has built up (through contributions and the investment return on these). This is known as your 'Protected Rights'. There is no GMP as such, but your Additional Pension will be reduced by an amount which may be more or less than the pension provided by your scheme.

Widows and widowers

A widow can inherit her husband's Additional Pension and add it on to her own. However, this cannot add up to more than the maximum Additional Pension a single person can receive. Adjustments will be made for periods contracted out of SERPS. A widow is entitled to half of her husband's GMP (if he was a member of a COSR scheme). She will receive half (or in certain situations all) of the Protected Rights if he belonged to a COMP or approved personal pension scheme.

These rules also apply to a widower if his wife dies when they are both over pension age (60 for women, 65 for men).

Social security guide NP 46 gives more details about the calculation. Leaflet NP 38 or form BR 19 explains how to apply for a statement of your Additional Pension.

GRADUATED PENSION (TAXABLE)

This pension scheme existed from April 1961 to April 1975 and was based on graduated contributions paid from earnings. If you were over 18 during this period and paying graduated contributions, your Graduated Pension (also known as Graduated Retirement Benefit) for the year 1993–94 will be based on the rates shown below:

Women   7.35p for every £9.00 contributions paid

Men   7.35p for every £7.50 contributions paid

This will be paid when you claim your pension, normally with the Basic Pension. However, you can receive Graduated Pension even if you do not qualify for a Basic Pension.

Married women, widows and widowers

If you are a married woman of 60 or more and your husband has put off drawing his pension, you should be aware that any Graduated Pension you receive – however little – may mean you will not benefit from an increased married woman's pension when your husband draws his pension. See page 27 for further information.

A widow can inherit half her late husband's Graduated Pension, as can a widower whose wife died after 5 April 1979, provided they were both over pension age (60 for women, 65 for men) when she died.

OVER-80s PENSION (TAXABLE)

This is a non-contributory Retirement Pension of £33.70 a week for people aged 80 and over who have no Retirement Pension. For someone who already gets a Retirement Pension of less than £33.70 a week, an Over-80s Pension will be paid to bring that pension up to this level.

To qualify for this pension you have to be living in the United Kingdom on the day you became 80 or the date of your claim if this is later, and to have been here for ten years or more in any 20-year period after your 60th birthday. If you have lived in Gibraltar or another member of the European Community, this may help you satisfy the conditions.

The Over-80s Pension will be counted as income in full for the purposes of Income Support, Housing Benefit and Council Tax Benefit.

See social security leaflet NI 184.

AGE-RELATED ADDITIONS (TAXABLE)

Once you reach 80 you will receive an extra 25p with your Retirement Pension. If a husband and wife are both over 80 they will each receive an extra 25p.

If you were receiving Invalidity Benefit before you started to draw your pension, any Invalidity Allowance you were receiving will continue to be paid with your pension. This will be known as 'Invalidity Addition'. (See pp 86–90 for more about Invalidity Benefit.)

GOING ON WORKING

This section looks at the choices open to people who wish to work after reaching pension age (60 for women, 65 for men). People can choose to claim their pension or to defer it (that is, put off drawing it) in order to gain increases later on.

Working and drawing the State Pension

Once you reach pension age, you can draw your State Pension if you satisfy the contribution conditions. It will not be affected by the amount you earn or the number of hours you work. You should note, however, that if you are claiming an addition with your pension for a dependent husband or wife, this addition could be affected by their earnings, as explained on page 11.

Although your pension will not be reduced because you are working, it is counted as part of your taxable income. Your tax code will be adjusted to take into account any pension (including Additional and Graduated) you receive.

If you carry on working after pension age, you will not have to pay NI contributions. You should receive a certificate of exemption from the DSS to give to your employer, who will still have to pay contributions for you.

Deferring your pension

You can choose to defer drawing your pension for a period of up to five years after pension age in order to earn extra pension.

You cannot normally defer a pension after the age of 65 (women) or 70 (men). However, you may be able to defer your pension if you are a married woman of 65 or over with a husband under 70 who is deferring his pension, as explained below. The period for which you defer your pension will be called 'the period of enhancement'.

You do not have to be working to defer your pension but you will not be counted as having deferred your pension if you are receiving certain other benefits instead. For example, a man who decides not to draw his pension at the age of 65 but to continue to claim Invalidity Benefit until the age of 70 will not gain any extra pension.

Even if you start drawing your pension, it is possible to change your mind and defer it instead. However, this can only be done once. If you are a married man and your wife is drawing a pension based on your contributions, you may need your wife's consent before cancelling your pension as she will have to give hers up too.

Extra Basic Pension

If you defer your pension, it will be increased by about 7.5 per cent a year for each full year that you do not draw it. (If you were deferring your pension before 6 April 1979, you will have earned a smaller increase.) For each week that you defer your pension, it will be increased by 1/7p in the pound, but you must defer it for at least seven weeks to gain any increase.

If you put off drawing your pension for the full five years, it will be increased by about 37.5 per cent. For example, in April 1993, the Basic Pension of £56.10 a week would be increased to £77.02 a week for someone who had deferred it for five years.

See social security leaflets N1 92 and NP 46.

Extra Additional and Graduated Pension

If you defer drawing your pension, your Additional and Graduated Pensions will be increased in the same way as, the Basic Pension.

See social security guide NP 46 for information about the effect of deferring your pension on an occupational pension.

Extra pension for married women

If you are a married woman entitled to a pension on your own contributions and you defer retirement, the pension will be increased as described previously.

If you are aged 60–64 and entitled to a pension on your husband's contributions, you can defer this to gain an increase. If you are 60 or over and your husband is deferring his pension, you will not be able to draw the married woman's pension. Once he draws his pension, you will both receive increases.

However, your pension on your husband's contributions will not be increased if, while your husband is deferring his pension, you draw another benefit such as Additional Pension or Graduated Pension. It may be better not to draw, for example, a small Additional Pension if your husband is deferring his retirement.

A test case in 1992 established that women drawing a small Graduated Pension while their husband deferred his pension should still have been able to gain increases and as a consequence the rules were changed to the position described above. Women entitled to extra pension as a result of the case should have been traced. If you started to draw Graduated Pension but not any Basic Pension before 5 August 1992 and your husband was 65 or over and deferring his pension, you can contact Age Concern England for further information about whether you might be affected by the test case.

Unemployment and sickness

If you are a man under 70 or a woman under 65 and have put off drawing your pension, you can claim Unemployment Benefit or Sickness Benefit in the normal way, provided you would have been entitled to a Retirement Pension had you chosen to draw it or you are ill owing to an industrial accident or an industrial disease. Information about Sickness Benefit is given on pages 84–85.

The basic weekly rates of Unemployment Benefit for people over pension age (60 for women, 65 for men) are shown below:

Claimant	£56.10
Adult dependant	£33.70

You will also get increases for any Additional Pension and Graduated Pension you have earned up to pension age. If you are only entitled to a reduced pension, your Unemployment or Sickness Benefit will also be reduced. More information about Unemployment Benefit and the rates for people under pension age is given on the following page.

The weeks spent claiming Unemployment Benefit or Sickness Benefit do not count towards extra pension when you do finally claim your pension.

EARLY RETIREMENT

This section summarises the benefits available to older people who leave work before pension age (60 for women, 65 for men) and explains how to ensure that your Retirement Pension is protected.

Unemployment Benefit (taxable)

This benefit depends on your having paid sufficient NI contributions. It can be paid for up to 52 weeks. To qualify you must be unemployed and 'actively seeking work'. The weekly rates for someone under pension age are shown below:

Claimant	£44.65
Adult dependant	£27.55

However, if you are 55 or over and have an occupational or personal pension of more than £35 a week, your Unemployment Benefit is reduced by 10p for every 10p over £35. If you have an adult dependant such as a husband or wife, you can claim the addition of £27.55 as long as he or she does not earn more than £27.55 a week or receive that amount from certain social security benefits.

You may be disqualified from Unemployment Benefit for up to 26 weeks if you leave a job voluntarily without 'just cause'. You may be disqualified if you choose to accept early retirement but not if you are made redundant. If you are disqualified from benefit, ask for advice from a Citizens Advice Bureau or advice agency.

See social security leaflet NI 12.

Sickness and Invalidity Benefit

If you are unable to work because of sickness and are no longer employed you may be entitled to Sickness Benefit for up to 28 weeks and then Invalidity Benefit, depending on your contribution record. Invalidity Benefit is explained on pages 86–90 and Sickness Benefit on pages 84–85.

Income-related benefits

Whether or not you get any of the benefits described above, you may be entitled to Income Support, Housing Benefit and/or Council Tax Benefit, depending on your savings and income. These benefits are described in the section starting on page 37.

Occupational and personal pensions

You may qualify for an occupational pension before pension age (60 for women, 65 for men) if you retire early. You should check with your employer for details. You can draw a personal pension any time after you have reached the age of 50.

Protecting your State Pension

To make sure that you have paid enough contributions to receive a full pension when you reach pension age, check your contribution record by contacting your local Benefits Agency (social security) office.

You will receive credits towards your pension if you are drawing a benefit such as Unemployment or Invalidity Benefit. If you are under 60 and seeking work, it may be worth signing on as unemployed – even if you are not entitled to benefit – because you will receive credits. If you are a man aged 60–64, you will normally receive credits automatically even if you are not ill or signing on as unemployed. However, you cannot get these automatic credits for any tax year during which you are abroad for more than six months. If you are not entitled to credits and have an incomplete NI record, you may want to consider paying voluntary contributions.

WIDOW'S PAYMENT AND WIDOW'S PENSION

This section is aimed at older women, so a woman widowed under the age of 55 or with dependent children should seek further information. The two benefits described both depend on the husband's contribution record.

Widow's Payment (not taxable)

This is a single lump-sum payment of £1,000; it was introduced in April 1988 and is paid mainly to widows under the age of 60. If you are 60 or over when your husband dies, you will still receive the payment provided he was under 65 or he was over 65 but not drawing the State Retirement Pension. For example, you can receive the payment if your husband had deferred drawing his pension because he was working or drawing Invalidity Benefit.

Widow's Pension (taxable)

If you were aged 55–64 when your husband died (and you had not started to receive a Retirement Pension), you can receive a Widow's Pension of up to £56.10 a week. If your husband had not paid sufficient contributions, you may not get the full amount. You may also receive an Additional Pension based on your husband's earnings since April 1978 but not for any time when your husband was contracted out of SERPS. Instead, you will normally receive a pension from your husband's occupational or personal pension scheme.

When you reach pension age (60), you can draw the State Pension instead of the Widow's Pension or you can remain on the Widow's Pension until you reach 65. The amounts will often be the same, but you may also receive some Graduated Pension with the State Pension.

The Widow's Pension will not be affected by your earnings. However, if you do not draw your Retirement Pension at the age of 60, you will not earn extra pension unless you give up the Widow's Pension.

If you remarry, you will lose the Widow's Pension. It will also be suspended during any period when you live with a man as his wife. However, a woman of 60 or over who receives a Retirement Pension based on her previous husband's contribution will not lose this if she remarries.

See social security guide NP 45.

CHRISTMAS BONUS

The bonus of £10 will be paid to people who are entitled to one of the State benefits listed below and who are living in the United Kingdom or any European Community country during the week beginning 6 December 1993. The bonus is tax-free and has no effect on other benefits.

Who qualifies?

You will get the Christmas Bonus if you are receiving a Retirement Pension; Over-80s or Widow's Pension; Attendance Allowance; Disability Living Allowance (any level or component); Invalid Care Allowance; Invalidity Pension; Severe Disablement Allowance; Income Support, provided you have reached pension age (60 for women, 65 for men); War Widow's Pension; Unemployability Supplement or Allowance; Constant Attendance Allowance paid with a War or Industrial Disablement Pension. It is also payable to someone who receives a War Disablement Pension but does not get a qualifying social security benefit if they have reached 65 (women) or 70 (men).

Only one bonus can be given to each person. However, someone over pension age receiving it may get an additional bonus for a dependent spouse or an unmarried partner who is over pension age or who reaches pension age during the week beginning 6 December 1993 but is not entitled to the bonus in his or her own right (subject to the residency conditions described above).

How it is paid

There is usually no need to claim, as the bonus is paid automatically. Depending on the way your pension is normally paid, the bonus will be included in your order book, paid into a bank or building society account, or sent by giro cheque. If you think you are entitled to the bonus but do not receive it by the end of December, inform your local Benefits Agency (social security) office.

REVIEWS AND APPEALS

This section gives brief details about what to do if you disagree with a decision about a benefit or pension. It applies to many benefits but not to discretionary Social Fund payments, Housing Benefit, Council Tax Benefit or the medical conditions for disability benefits. For more information, see the relevant sections.

Most social security decisions are made by adjudication officers. If you disagree with one of their decisions, you can ask for it to be reviewed or take an appeal to a Social Security Appeal Tribunal (SSAT), which is independent of the DSS. There are also 'Secretary of State decisions', as explained below.

When you receive information about whether you have been awarded a benefit and how much you will get, you should also receive details about what to do if you disagree with the decision. If you want to challenge this, it is often useful to get advice from a local agency such as a Citizens Advice Bureau. They may be able to help you write to the DSS, prepare your case, or perhaps represent you at a tribunal.

Reviews

You can ask for a decision about your benefit to be reviewed at any time, if you think that the adjudication officer did not have all the facts or misunderstood the information supplied, if your circumstances have changed, or if you think the decision is incorrect for any other reason. Write to the local Benefits Agency (social security) office, asking for your case to be reviewed and giving your reasons. If the request for a review is turned down, you can appeal against this decision.

Appeals

If you want to appeal, write to the local Benefits Agency (social security) office within three months of receiving the letter giving the decision. If you appeal after this, you will need to explain why your appeal is late. The appeal will then go ahead if the tribunal chairman accepts there were good reasons for the delay. When you write, you should say which decision you wish to appeal against, and why you think the decision is wrong. Sometimes the adjudication officer may be able to change the decision on the basis of this information.

The tribunal

After writing your letter, you will be sent a copy of all the documents relevant to your case and details of where and when the tribunal will take place. Each case will be assessed by three people not connected with the DSS. There will also be an adjudication officer present.

When you arrive at the tribunal, a clerk will explain the procedures, which are intended to be as informal as possible. You will be given time to put your case and the tribunal will ask questions. The clerk should reimburse your travel expenses before you leave. The tribunal must decide whether the adjudication officer made the right decision according to the law, but cannot change a decision just because it seems unfair. You may be told the outcome straight away; otherwise the decision will be sent to you later.

Secretary of State decisions

Certain decisions are made on behalf of the Secretary of State, such as the number of NI contributions you have made or how benefits are paid. If you disagree with this type of decision, you can ask for it to be reconsidered. You should write to the local Benefits Agency (social security) office giving the reasons why you disagree.

See social security leaflet NI 246 or the detailed guide NI 260.

OCCUPATIONAL PENSIONS

This section summarises how occupational and personal pensions can affect the State benefits you receive. It is not within the scope of this book to give information about the different types of pension scheme, but details are given on how to obtain further information or deal with problems that arise.

How State benefits are affected

In general the State Pensions and other benefits will not be affected by an occupational or personal pension. However, an occupational or personal pension will be counted as income in full for the purposes of Income Support, Housing Benefit and Council Tax Benefit. It can also reduce the amount of Unemployment Benefit you get if you are 55 or over, as explained on page 29. If you receive Invalidity Benefit, once you reach pension age (60 for women, 65 for men) any Additional Pension paid with your benefit will be reduced if you were contracted out of the State Additional Pension scheme and contributing to an occupational or approved personal pension instead (see pp 86–90 for more about Invalidity Benefit).

If you receive a pension or benefit and wish to claim an increase for a dependent wife or husband, any occupational or personal pension they receive will be counted as earnings and may affect your increase, as explained on page 11.

Advice about occupational and personal pensions

If you have a problem relating to an occupational or personal pension scheme that you cannot sort out with your employer or pension provider, you can contact the Occupational Pensions Advisory Service (OPAS, 11 Belgrave Road, London SW1V 1RB) or a Citizens Advice Bureau. OPAS is an independent voluntary organisation with a network of local advisers who can offer free help and advice. If OPAS cannot resolve your problem they may suggest that a complaint is made to the Pensions Ombudsman.

In the summer of 1993 Age Concern is publishing *The Pensions Handbook*, which aims to provide an easily understandable guide to pension schemes. Contact the Publications Department at Age Concern England for more details.

Income-Related (Means-Tested) Benefits

This part of Your Rights *describes benefits that older people may be able to claim depending on their income and savings. It covers Income Support, Housing Benefit and Council Tax Benefit, which help with regular weekly expenses, and the Social Fund, which provides lump-sum payments for exceptional expenses. Many older people do not claim the income-related benefits they are entitled to, so you should make sure you are not losing out.*

INCOME SUPPORT

This benefit helps with weekly basic living expenses by topping up your income to a level set by the Government. You do not need to have paid NI contributions to qualify for Income Support, but your income and savings will be taken into account. Income Support replaced Supplementary Benefit in April 1988. It is not taxable provided you are aged 60 or over or can receive Income Support without being available for work.

If you receive Income Support, you are also likely to qualify for Housing Benefit and/or Council Tax Benefit, which are based on similar rules. These benefits help with rent and Council Tax payments. If your income is too high for you to qualify for Income Support, you may still be entitled to Housing Benefit and Council Tax Benefit.

Income Support can be paid to home-owners, tenants, and people in other circumstances such as living with family or friends. Once you get Income Support, you may also get other benefits such as the automatic right to free dental treatment (see pp 111–112), lump-sum payments from the Social Fund (see pp 51–53) and grants for insulation (see p 99).

See social security guide IS 20 for detailed information.

Who qualifies?

You may receive Income Support if your savings are £8,000 or less, you have a low income, and neither you nor your partner works 16 hours a week or more. If you are under 60 and able to work, you will not normally be able to claim Income Support unless you are signing on as unemployed and actively seeking work.

A 'partner' is your husband or wife or someone you live with as though you were married. Throughout this section the word 'partner' will be used instead of 'spouse' because you do not have to be married to be treated as a couple. You apply for Income Support for yourself and your partner. If you live with someone else such as a friend, you can both apply for Income Support separately.

How to work it out

Income Support is worked out by using the following steps, which are explained below.

1 Add up the value of your savings.

2 Add up your weekly income, but note that certain kinds of income are ignored.

3 Work out the amount the Government says you need to live on, called the 'applicable amount'.

4 Compare your applicable amount with your income to see whether you are entitled to benefit.

1 Your savings

If your savings are more than £8,000, you cannot get Income Support. For a couple, savings are added together, but the limit is the same. The term 'savings' is used here to cover both capital and savings.

If you have savings of between £3,000 and £8,000, an income of £1 a week for every £250 (or part of £250) over £3,000 will be counted. For example, savings of £3,480 will be counted as an income of £2 a week; savings of £5,760 will be counted as £12 a week. This is called 'tariff income'. Savings of £3,000 or less will not affect your benefit.

■ If you 'deprive' yourself of savings in order to get benefit or increase the amount, you may be considered as still having those savings. Depriving yourself of savings might include giving money to your family or buying expensive items in order to gain benefit. You should seek advice if you are refused benefit because of this.

Savings and capital are normally valued at their current market or surrender value. If there are expenses involved in selling them, 10 per cent will be deducted. Most forms of savings and capital will be taken into account including:

- cash;
- bank and building society accounts (including current accounts that do not pay interest);
- National Savings accounts and certificates (valued according to rules which the local Benefits Agency (social security) office will explain);
- premium bonds;
- stocks and shares;
- half of any joint savings you have with another person (eg a joint account with your son or daughter).

Some types of savings will be ignored including:

- the value of your home if you own it and are living there;
- the surrender value of a life assurance policy;
- arrears of certain benefits such as Attendance Allowance or Income Support for up to 52 weeks;
- your personal possessions, unless they have been bought in order to reduce your savings.

2 Your income

Income includes earnings, State benefits, occupational or personal pensions and any other money you have coming in after tax and NI contributions have been paid. For a couple, the income of both partners is added together when calculating Income Support.

However, some income may be fully or partly ignored when the Benefits Agency (social security) office works out your benefit.

Income that will be fully ignored includes:

- Housing Benefit and Council Tax Benefit;
- the mobility component of the Disability Living Allowance;
- Attendance Allowance and the care component of the Disability Living Allowance, although there are special rules for people in residential or nursing homes, as explained on pages 106–107;
- actual interest or income from savings or capital under £8,000 (only tariff income will be counted, as explained above). Interest is not counted as income but once it is paid into an account it will be counted as part of your savings;
- the special war widow's pension introduced in April 1990 for 'pre-1973 widows', which is now £47.84 (in addition to the £10 of a War Widow's Pension outlined below).

The following are examples of parts of weekly income that will also be ignored:

- £5 of your earnings if you work;
- £5 of your partner's earnings from work;
- £15 of earnings if you work and you are a carer receiving the carer premium or in certain circumstances when you or your partner are disabled (instead of the £5 listed above);
- £10 of a War Widow's Pension or War Disablement Pension;
- £10 of regular payments from a friend, relative or charity (but this £10 will not be ignored on top of £10 from a war pension because the total amount from these two types of income that can be ignored must not be more than £10);
- £4 rent from a subtenant living in your home;
- £12.60 from a subtenant whose rent includes a heating charge;
- £20 income from a boarder plus half of the boarder's charge over £20.

Having decided what kinds of income will be ignored, add up the rest of your income, including tariff income for savings between £3,000 and £8,000. The total is the weekly income used to work out your Income Support.

3 Your applicable amount

This is the amount of money the Government says you need to live on each week. It is worked out by adding together the personal allowance and any premiums that apply to you. Premiums are awarded depending on your age and whether you are disabled. For Income Support certain housing costs for home-owners can also be included, as explained on pages 47–48. Allowances and premiums for children are not covered here. Once you have worked out your applicable amount you will be able to check whether you are likely to qualify for one or more of the income-related benefits (Income Support, Housing Benefit and Council Tax Benefit).

Personal allowances

The personal allowances for people over 25 are shown below:

| Single person | £44.00 |
| Couple | £69.00 |

Premiums

These premiums are part of the system of income-related benefits. You must add these to your personal allowance to see if you qualify for Income Support, Housing Benefit and/or Council Tax Benefit. The six premiums described here are the ones that apply to people aged 60 or more, disabled people and carers. You can only be awarded one out of the following premiums: pensioner premium, enhanced pensioner premium, higher pensioner premium and disability premium.

If you fulfil the conditions for more than one of these, you will be awarded whichever is higher. However, the severe disability premium can be given on top of the disability or higher pensioner premium, and the carer premium will be awarded along with any other premiums.

Pensioner premium

If you are single and aged 60–74, you will get this premium (unless you qualify for the higher pensioner premium described below). For a couple, you must both be under 75 and one or both of you must be 60 or over. The rates are shown below:

Single person   £17.30
Couple   £26.25

Enhanced pensioner premium
This is awarded to single people aged 75–79 and to couples when one or both are 75–79 and both are under 80. The rates are shown below:

Single person   £19.30
Couple   £29.00

Higher pensioner premium
You will get this if you are aged 80 or more or if you are aged 60–79 and fulfil the disability conditions for a disability premium (see below). For a couple, only one of you needs to fulfil either of these conditions. The rates are shown below:

Single person   £23.55
Couple   £33.70

Disability premium
This is given to disabled people under 60. To be counted as 'disabled' you must normally be getting a disability benefit such as Attendance Allowance, Disability Living Allowance (any level or component), Severe Disablement Allowance or Invalidity Benefit or be registered as blind. For a couple, only one of you needs to fulfil these conditions. The rates are shown below:

Single person   £18.45
Couple   £26.45

People may also be able to receive the disability premium in some situations where they have been unable to work for at least 28 weeks but do not receive one of the disability benefits outlined above. (You cannot qualify for the higher pensioner premium in this way.)

Severe disability premium

Single people will get this provided they 'live alone' (but see below for exceptions to this) and receive Attendance Allowance or the middle or higher level of the care component of Disability Living Allowance (DLA), with no one receiving Invalid Care Allowance for looking after them. However, there are exceptions to the living alone rule: for example, you can still get this premium if you live with someone who also gets Attendance Allowance (or the middle or higher level of the care component of DLA), or with someone who is registered blind, or with a paid helper supplied by a charity, or in some cases where you are a joint tenant or joint owner and share the housing costs. If you are not sure if you qualify seek further advice, as the rules can be complicated.

If you are a couple you can normally only receive this premium if you both get Attendance Allowance (or the middle or higher level of the care component of DLA) and you are 'living alone' as described above. You will get the higher rate if neither of you has a carer receiving Invalid Care Allowance (ICA) and the single rate if you both get Attendance Allowance (or the middle or higher level of the care component of DLA) and just one of you has a carer getting ICA. The rates are shown below:

Single person	£33.70
Couple, one person qualifying	£33.70
Couple, both qualifying	£67.40

■ Remember you can get this premium as well as either the disability or the higher pensioner premium.

Carer premium

This premium is given to carers who are receiving Invalid Care Allowance (ICA). It will also be given to people who applied for ICA on or after 1 October 1990 and fulfil all the conditions but cannot receive it because they are getting another benefit instead.

For example, if you are receiving a Widow's Pension of £56.10, you will not be paid ICA as well. However, if you apply for ICA, you may receive a letter saying you are entitled to ICA but cannot be paid it, which you can show to the Benefits Agency (social security) office (for Income Support) or the council (for Housing and Council Tax Benefit), who will award you the premium.

The carer premium can continue to be paid for eight weeks after the person you care for dies, or you cease being a carer for some other reason. A change in the rules in April 1993 means that someone getting the carer premium can now have earnings from work of £15 a week without losing benefit. The rates for the carer premium are as follows:

Single person	£11.95
Couple, one person qualifying	£11.95
Couple, both receiving ICA	£23.90

■ Warning If the person you care for receives the severe disability premium (see above), they will lose this if you are awarded ICA. You might be able to receive an extra £11.95 a week through the carer premium while the person you care for would lose a premium worth £33.70. If you are not sure whether to claim ICA or not, get advice first.

4 Calculating Income Support

Once you have worked out your applicable amount by adding together your personal allowance and any premiums, compare this figure with your income. If your income is less than your applicable amount, you will qualify for Income Support (depending on your savings). If your income is more, you will not get Income Support but you may get Housing Benefit and/or Council Tax Benefit.

Example

Rose is aged 76, and lives alone in a council flat. Her only income is the State Pension of £56.10 a week. She has savings of £350.

Rose adds up her income

Retirement Pension	£56.10
total	£56.10

Rose adds up her applicable amount

Personal allowance	£44.00
Enhanced pensioner premium	£19.30
total	£63.30

Rose's income of £56.10 a week is less than her applicable amount of £63.30. The difference is £7.20. This is how much Income Support she will get on top of her Retirement Pension.

Rose will also get Housing Benefit and Council Tax Benefit to cover all her rent and Council Tax.

Example

Bill and Mary are a married couple in their 60s. Their joint State Pensions come to £90 and Bill gets a small pension of £13 a week from his old job. They live in their own home and they have savings of £3,800. Mary suffers with rheumatoid arthritis and gets Attendance Allowance.

Bill and Mary add up their income, ignoring Mary's Attendance Allowance

State Pension	£90.00
Work pension	£13.00
Weekly tariff income from savings	£4.00
total	£107.00

Bill and Mary add up their applicable amount

Personal allowance	£69.00
Higher pensioner premium	£33.70
total	£102.70

Their income is £4.30 a week more than their applicable amount, so they do not qualify for Income Support. But they should claim Council Tax Benefit to get help with their Council Tax payments.

Help with housing costs

In addition to your personal allowance and any premiums, your Income Support applicable amount can include an addition for certain housing costs. This mainly applies to home-owners as rent and service charges for tenants are covered by Housing Benefit. If your housing costs are considered 'excessive' (taking into account your situation), the amount added to the applicable amount may be restricted. The housing costs which can be included are:

- mortgage interest (but if you are under 60 the help is restricted to 50 per cent of the interest for the first 16 weeks of a claim);
- interest on a loan for certain repairs or improvements (with the same restriction as for mortgage interest);
- ground rent;
- certain service charges.

Deductions for people living in your home

The help with housing costs may be reduced if there is someone else living in your home apart from your partner or a dependent child. This is because people such as grown-up sons and daughters (sometimes called 'non-dependants') are expected to contribute to housing costs. However, no reduction will be made if you or your partner are blind or you or your partner receive Attendance Allowance or the care component of Disability Living Allowance.

The deductions made will depend on the circumstances of the person living with you. If he or she is aged 18 or over, works 16 hours a week or more, and has an income of at least £70 a week, there are the following three rates:

Gross income of non-dependant	Weekly deduction
£70.00 to £104.99	£8.00
£105.00 to £134.99	£12.00
£135.00 or more	£21.00

For others aged 18 or over or people on Income Support aged 25 or over the deduction will be £4, while there is no deduction if the non-dependant is under 25 and receiving Income Support. If there is a couple living with you, only one deduction will be made.

Example

Mr and Mrs Wilson (both aged 65) have a mortgage. They pay £20 a week mortgage interest, so their applicable amount is worked out in the following way:

Personal allowance for a couple	£69.00
Pensioner premium	£26.25
Weekly mortgage interest	£20.00
total	£115.25

Their daughter who is 20 and earns £100 a week comes to live with them. There will therefore be a deduction of £8 from the amount allowed for mortgage interest. Their total Income Support rate will then be reduced to £107.25.

Income Support for people in different circumstances

Living in someone else's home

If you live in someone else's home as a member of their household – for example, with your son or daughter – Income Support will be worked out in the normal way. However, if your son or daughter gets help with housing costs through Income Support, Housing Benefit and/or Council Tax Benefit, this may be reduced because you are living there.

Boarders and hostel dwellers

If you are living in a hotel, guest house or hostel, or in board and lodgings, Income Support will be worked out in the normal way. You can claim Housing Benefit towards the rental element of your charges and some services. You will have to pay for meals, fuel and other items that are not covered by Housing Benefit from your weekly Income Support.

If you go into hospital

Income Support is reduced after six weeks if either you or your partner goes into hospital. If you are single, the personal allowance will be reduced to £14.05. You will not get any premiums, but you will still get housing costs. If you have a partner, you will get the normal amount minus £11.20.

After 52 weeks in hospital, a single person will have an applicable amount of £11.20 but no housing costs. If you have a partner, your personal allowance will be £11.20 and he or she will be assessed separately.

Residential and nursing homes

Income Support for people in residential or nursing homes is described on pages 101–104.

How to claim Income Support

You will need a claim form from the local Benefits Agency (social security) office. You can obtain this by calling in, writing, telephoning or sending in the tear-off slip from form IS 1, which you can get at the local Benefits Agency (social security) office or post office. If you need help with filling in the claim form, ask at the Benefits Agency, a Citizens Advice Bureau or a welfare rights advice agency.

Income Support is normally added to your Retirement Pension and paid in one order book. It cannot normally be paid directly into a bank at present. However, it may soon be possible to choose to receive Income Support paid directly into a bank or building society account.

Is it the wrong amount?

If you disagree with a decision that has been made about your Income Support (eg you may have been refused a premium), you can ask for the case to be reviewed or appeal against the decision (see pp 33–34). You also have the right to ask for more detailed information about why a decision was made.

THE SOCIAL FUND

The Social Fund provides lump-sum payments to people with low incomes in order to meet exceptional expenses. There are Funeral Payments, as described below, and Cold Weather Payments, which are explained on page 97. If you have other expenses, you may get help from the Discretionary Social Fund, which gives Community Care Grants and Budgeting or Crisis Loans.

The £1,000 capital limit for Social Fund payments described here applies only to people aged 60 and over. For younger people, a capital limit of £500 applies.

Funeral Payments

If you are responsible for the cost of a funeral and you or your partner are receiving Income Support, Housing Benefit, Council Tax Benefit or Disability Working Allowance, you can apply to the Social Fund for a payment to cover the basic costs of a simple funeral.

If you and/or your partner are aged 60 or over and have savings over £1,000, this will be taken into account, as will any money from the estate of the person who died or money from insurance policies. For example, if you have £1,300, you will be expected to put the first £300 towards the funeral, and you can then get help with the rest of the cost.

To make a claim you will need form SF 200 from your local Benefits Agency (social security) office. You normally have to claim within three months of the funeral, but, if possible, check what you are entitled to before arranging a funeral.

See social security leaflet D 49 for what to do after a death.

The Discretionary Social Fund

The payments described below are different from most other social security benefits in that they are discretionary, and, except for Community Care Grants, they are loans which have to be repaid. There is a limited budget for the Social Fund which restricts the number of payments that can be made. There is a legal framework for the system and the Social Fund officers have a book of guidance which helps them make decisions. They must consider the needs of the people who apply and decide which of these can be met from the budget.

Community Care Grants

These are available to people on Income Support, and the grants do not have to be repaid. For applicants aged 60 or over, savings over £1,000 will be deducted from any grant awarded. For example, if you have £1,100 savings and you need an item costing £300 you would only be able to be given a grant for £200. If you are not sure whether you will get help, you have nothing to lose by applying. It is important to include all the relevant information (see below on 'How to apply').

There are four sorts of grant:

- help with moving out of institutional or residential care (eg for a bed, a cooker, fuel connection or removal costs);
- help to enable you to remain living at home (eg for minor house repairs, bedding and essential furniture, removal costs to more suitable accommodation);
- help with exceptional pressures on families caused by disability, chronic sickness or a breakdown in a relationship;
- help with certain travel expenses (eg for visiting someone who is ill or attending a relative's funeral).

Budgeting Loans

These are available to people who have been on Income Support for at least 26 weeks and need items they cannot afford. The loans, which are interest-free, will have to be repaid, and any savings over £1,000 (£500 for people under 60) will reduce the amount of the loan.

Items you may get a loan for include: costs of an essential move to more suitable accommodation, redecoration costs, clothing or furniture. You will be more likely to get a loan for something considered a high priority such as bedding than for an item with a lower priority.

Crisis Loans

These interest-free loans are available to anyone (not just people on Income Support) who needs money urgently in an emergency or has been involved in a disaster (eg fire or flood). The Social Fund officer will take into account all your family's savings and income which are available to you. You may be able to get a loan provided this is the only way of preventing serious risk to your health or safety or that of a member of your family.

Repayment of loans

Budgeting or Crisis Loans will only be awarded if the officer thinks you will be able to repay them. Normally repayments will be deducted from your benefit and loans should be repaid within 78 weeks. In special circumstances the repayment period will be extended to 104 weeks.

The repayment rates will be fixed after taking into account your income and your existing and future commitments. In the case of Crisis Loans, repayments will not normally begin until after the period of crisis is over.

How to apply

To apply for a Community Care Grant or Budgeting Loan, you need application form SF 300 from your local Benefits Agency (social security) office. If you need a Crisis Loan, ask at the office.

You should give as much information as possible about your circumstances and why you need help (eg health problems). If there is not enough room on the form, use a separate sheet.

You may also wish to include a letter of support from your GP or social worker. A welfare rights agency or Citizens Advice Bureau may be able to help you with the application.

If you are unhappy about a decision

Community Care Grants and loans from the Social Fund are discretionary payments. If you disagree with a decision, you cannot appeal to a Social Security Appeal Tribunal, but instead there is a special system of review. The first stage of review is at the local office, and you are given the chance to put your case personally to a Social Fund officer. If you are still dissatisfied, you can take your case to a Social Fund inspector, who is independent of your local Benefits Agency.

For the other payments from the Social Fund – Funeral and Cold Weather Payments – there is a right of appeal to a Social Security Appeal Tribunal.

See social security leaflet SFL 2 or detailed guide SB 16 for more information about the Social Fund.

HOUSING BENEFIT AND COUNCIL TAX BENEFIT (NOT TAXABLE)

Housing Benefit provides help with rent, with certain service charges and, in Northern Ireland, with general rates. People who live in Northern Ireland and require information about rate rebates should contact Age Concern Northern Ireland.

Council Tax Benefit is a social security benefit which provides help with paying the Council Tax. See also 'Help with the Council Tax' on pages 108–109, which gives information about other ways your Council Tax bill may be reduced which are not related to your income or savings.

Who qualifies for Housing Benefit?

You may get Housing Benefit if you have a low income, your savings are no more than £16,000, and you are responsible for paying rent. Benefit is available to council, housing association and private tenants and to people in the following circumstances:

Boarders and people living in hostels may get Housing Benefit for the accommodation part of their charges and may also get Income Support (see p 49).

People in private residential or nursing homes will not normally be able to receive Housing Benefit towards the home's fees unless they were receiving it on 29 October 1990. Someone living in a local authority home cannot get Housing Benefit.

People living in a houseboat may get benefit for the mooring charges.

People living in a caravan or mobile home may get help with the site charges.

Joint tenants may receive Housing Benefit towards the part of the costs for which they are responsible.

People living with a landlord who is a close relative may claim Housing Benefit if they live separately in self-contained accommodation. However, they cannot claim benefit if they are part of the same household, or if it is not a 'commercial arrangement'. Get advice if you are unsure about your position.

Who qualifies for Council Tax Benefit?

There are two types of Council Tax Benefit known as 'main Council Tax Benefit' and 'second adult rebate'. If you are liable to pay (responsible for paying) the Council Tax you may be able to receive main Council Tax Benefit provided you have no more than £16,000 savings and a low income. If you have a partner (that is, you are married or live with someone as though you were married), the amount of rebate you get will be worked out on your combined savings and income. If you are jointly responsible for a bill with someone other than your partner you can apply for help with your share of the tax.

The second adult rebate will be available to some people regardless of their income and savings in certain circumstances when they have one or more people with low incomes living with them. This is covered on page 65, while the rest of this section covers the main benefit scheme.

How to work out your benefit

Housing Benefit and Council Tax Benefit are worked out using similar calculations. The rules outlined below apply to both benefits unless stated otherwise. To work out how much benefit you will get, follow the steps listed, which are then explained.

1 Calculate the maximum weekly rent and Council Tax for which you can get benefit.
2 Deduct an amount for people living in your home.
3 Add up the value of your savings.

4 Add up your weekly income, but note that certain kinds of income are ignored.

5 Work out the amount the Government says you need to live on, called the 'applicable amount'.

6 Calculate your benefit according to the formula explained below.

7 For Housing Benefit, check that the benefit is above the minimum amount payable, which is 50p a week. There is no minimum payment for Council Tax Benefit.

1 Your rent and Council Tax

For Housing Benefit purposes, rent is the payment made to occupy your home. It also covers certain service charges – eg for furniture, cleaning communal areas, cleaning your rooms (if neither you nor your partner can do this), portering, entry phones, wardens and caretakers, rubbish removal. Also included in service charges is the cost of an emergency alarm system, but only if it has been installed in accommodation specially designed or adapted for older people or those with disabilities.

Water rates and sewerage charges are not included in the rent, and you cannot get benefit towards these. Home-owners cannot get Housing Benefit for service charges or mortgage payments; however, they may get help with these from Income Support (see pp 47–48).

The maximum Housing Benefit you can get is 100 per cent of your rent including service charges.

If the council considers that your rent is too high (taking into account your circumstances) or that the rent has increased unreasonably while you have been getting Housing Benefit, they may decide not to pay Housing Benefit on the extra amount you have to pay. If this is the case, you should get advice from a welfare rights or housing advice centre or a Citizens Advice Bureau.

The maximum Council Tax Benefit you can get is 100 per cent of your bill. (Under the Community Charge system nearly everyone had to pay at least 20 per cent of their bill but this is no longer the case.) The benefit is based on the amount you are asked to pay after any discounts or reductions have been given. For example, if you live alone you will receive a 25 per cent discount on your bill, and your benefit will be worked out after this has been deducted.

■ Note that the calculations in this section are all done on a weekly basis. So if you pay your Council Tax by ten monthly instalments, you will first have to work out how much this would be per week over the whole year.

Heating charges

Some people have a charge for heating included in their rent. You cannot get Housing Benefit for heating and other fuel charges. For example, if you pay £35 a week rent and £5 of that is for heating, you will only get a maximum of £30 Housing Benefit, as the charge for fuel will be deducted.

If your weekly fuel charges are not stated as a separate amount, the council will deduct the amounts listed below:

Heating	£8.60
Hot water	£1.05
Cooking	£1.05
Lighting	£0.70
All fuel	£11.40

The amounts are lower if you only have one room.

2 Deductions for people living in your home

A deduction will normally be made from your Housing Benefit and Council Tax Benefit if you have someone else living with you who is not your partner or a dependent child nor a joint tenant or joint owner. This is because people such as grown-up sons and daughters (sometimes called 'non-dependants') are expected to contribute to housing costs. However, no deduction will be made if you or your partner are blind or receive Attendance Allowance or the care component of Disability Living Allowance. There are also some types of non-dependant who do not give rise to a deduction – for example, students or people in hospital for more than six weeks.

If the person living with you is aged 18 or over, works 16 hours a week or more, and has a gross income of at least £70 a week there are the following three rates of deductions:

Gross income of non-dependant	Weekly deduction from rent	Weekly deduction from Council Tax
£70.00 to £104.99	£8.00	£1.00
£105.00 to £134.99	£12.00	£2.00
£135.00 or more	£21.00	£2.00

For rent there will be no deduction if the person who lives with you is under 25 and receiving Income Support, while there will be a £4 deduction for someone aged 25 on Income Support or for others aged 18 or over. For Council Tax Benefit there is no deduction for a non-dependant receiving Income Support while for others not working 16 hours a week or with an income of less than £105 there will be a £1 deduction.

Only one deduction is made for a couple living with you.

3 Your savings

If your savings are more than £16,000, you cannot get Housing Benefit or Council Tax Benefit. For a couple, savings are added together, but the limit is the same. The term 'savings' is used here to cover both capital and savings.

If you have savings of between £3,000 and £16,000 an income of £1 a week for every £250 (or part of £250) over £3,000 will be counted. For example, savings of £3,480 will be counted as an income of £2 a week. Savings of £10,760 will be counted as

£32 a week. This is called 'tariff income'. Savings of £3,000 or less will not affect your benefit.

■ If you 'deprive' yourself of savings in order to get benefit or increase the amount of benefit, you may be considered as still having those savings. Depriving yourself of savings might include giving money away to your family or buying expensive items in order to gain benefit. You should seek advice if you are refused benefit because of this.

Savings and capital are normally valued at their current market or surrender value. If there are expenses involved in selling them, 10 per cent will be deducted. Most forms of savings and capital will be taken into account, including:

- cash;
- bank and building society accounts (including current accounts that do not pay interest);
- National Savings accounts and certificates (valued according to rules which the local council will explain);
- premium bonds;
- stocks and shares;
- half of any joint savings you have with another person (eg a joint account with your son or daughter).

Some types of savings and capital will be ignored, including:

- the value of your home if you own it and are living there;
- the surrender value of a life assurance policy;
- arrears of certain benefits such as Attendance Allowance or Income Support for up to 52 weeks;
- your personal possessions (unless they have been bought in order to reduce your savings).

4 Your income

Income includes earnings, State benefits, occupational or personal pensions and any other money you have coming in after tax and NI contributions have been paid. For a couple, the income of both partners is added together when calculating benefit.

However, some income may be fully or partly ignored when your benefit is calculated. Income that will be fully ignored includes:

- Income Support;
- Disability Living Allowance;
- Attendance Allowance;
- actual interest or income from savings or capital under £16,000 (only tariff income will be counted, as explained above). Interest is not counted as income, but once it is paid into an account it will be counted as part of your savings;
- the special war widow's pension introduced in April 1990 for 'pre-1973 widows', which is now £47.84 (in addition to the £10 of a War Widow's Pension outlined below).

The following are examples of parts of weekly income that will also be ignored:

- £5 of your earnings if you work and are single;
- £10 of your or your partner's earnings from work;
- £15 of earnings if you work and you are a carer receiving the carer premium or in certain circumstances when you or your partner are disabled (instead of the £5 or £10 listed above);
- £10 of a War Widow's Pension or War Disablement Pension (the council has the discretion to increase the amount from these pensions that is ignored when working out your benefit, but not all councils operate such schemes);
- £10 of regular payments from a friend, relative or charity (but this £10 will not be ignored on top of £10 from a war pension because the total amount from these two types of income that can be ignored must not be more than £10);
- £4 rent from a subtenant living in your home;
- £12.60 from a subtenant whose rent includes a heating charge;

- £20 income from a boarder plus half of the boarder's charge over £20.

To work out your benefit, decide what kinds of income will be ignored and add up the remainder (including tariff income for savings between £3,000 and £16,000).

5 Your applicable amount

This is the amount of money the Government says someone needs to live on. If your income is higher than this, you may still get some help with rent and the Council Tax.

Your applicable amount for Housing Benefit and Council Tax Benefit is worked out in the same way as for Income Support except that there are no additions for the housing costs of home-owners. To work out your applicable amount add up the personal allowance and any premiums that apply to you (see pp 42–45).

6 Calculating Housing Benefit and Council Tax Benefit

Once you have worked out your applicable amount, compare this with your income. If your income is the *same as* or *less than* your applicable amount, you will normally get all your rent and Council Tax paid (unless there are deductions for other people living in your home).

If your income is *more than* your applicable amount, the maximum benefit you can get is reduced. You first work out the difference between your income and your applicable amount. The maximum Housing Benefit payable is reduced by 65 per cent of this difference. The maximum Council Tax Benefit is reduced by 20 per cent of the difference.

Another way of explaining the calculation is to say that your maximum Housing Benefit is reduced by 65p for every pound that your income is more than your applicable amount. Your maximum Council Tax Benefit is reduced by 20p for every pound that your income is more than your applicable amount.

Example

Miss Walker is aged 64 and lives alone. Her income consists of the State Pension (Basic and Additional Pension) of £62 a week and the mobility component of Disability Living Allowance of £31.40 a week. She has £500 savings and pays £35 a week rent and £5 a week Council Tax.

The maximum Housing Benefit she can get is £35 a week (100 per cent of her rent). The maximum Council Tax Benefit she can get is £5 a week (100 per cent of her Council Tax). There are no non-dependant deductions because she lives alone.

Her savings will not affect her benefit, and the total amount of her income counted will be £62 because her Disability Living Allowance is ignored.

Miss Walker's applicable amount is set out below

Personal allowance	£44.00
Higher pensioner premium	£23.55
total	£67.55

Her income is less than her applicable amount, so she will get the maximum Housing Benefit of £35 a week for rent and the maximum Council Tax Benefit of £5 a week. She will also qualify for Income Support and should make a claim.

Example

Mr and Mrs Khan are both aged 68 and live in a rented house. They pay £48 a week rent which includes £8 heating. Their Council Tax is £9 a week. They have a State Pension of £89.80 a week, Mr Khan's occupational pension of £23.45 a week, and savings of £3,400.

The maximum Housing Benefit they can get is £40 (£48 minus the heating charge of £8). The maximum Council Tax Benefit they can get is £9. They have nobody else living with them so there will be no non-dependant deductions.

Mr and Mrs Khan add up their income

State Pension	£89.80
Occupational pension	£23.45
Tariff income (for savings over £3,000)	£2.00
total	£115.25

They calculate their applicable amount

Personal allowance	£69.00
Pensioner premium	£26.25
total	£95.25

Their income is more than their applicable amount, the difference being £20 (£115.25–£95.25).

Their weekly benefit is worked out in the following way

Rent

100% of rent	£40.00
Less 65% of difference (65% of £20)	£13.00
Housing Benefit	£27.00

Council Tax

100% of charge	£9.00
Less 20% of difference (20% of £20)	£4.00
Council Tax Benefit	£5.00

Total benefit is

Housing Benefit	£27.00
Council Tax Benefit	£5.00

Mr and Mrs Khan will have to pay £13 a week for rent plus the £8 heating charge and £4 towards the Council Tax.

If their daughter who is 20, works full-time and earns £120 a week comes to live with them their Housing Benefit will be reduced by £12 and their Council Tax Benefit by £2 a week.

Second adult rebate

If you are liable to pay the Council Tax you might get a second adult rebate if one or more people with a low income live with you, regardless of the level of your savings and income. This will usually only apply to people who do not have a partner. You will get a 25 per cent rebate if you are responsible for the tax and one or more people receiving Income Support live with you. A 15 per cent rebate is given if the person or people living with you have a joint gross income of £105 or less, while there is a 7.5 per cent discount if their income is between £105 and £135. In assessing the income of people living with you no account is taken of Attendance Allowance, Disability Living Allowance or the income of anyone receiving Income Support.

Example

Mrs Grant is a widow who owns her own home. Her son is living with her and receives Income Support. Her Council Tax bill for the year is £400. She is not entitled to the main Council Tax Benefit because she has £18,000 savings. However, she applies for a rebate and receives the second adult rebate of 25 per cent (£100) on the basis of her son's low income.

Some people will be entitled to the main Council Tax Benefit and the second adult rebate. In this case the council will award you whichever benefit will give you the greater amount.

Only brief details have been given here as this system can be complicated, so contact your local council or advice agency if you need further information.

Benefit for people in different circumstances

Absence from home

If you are temporarily away from home, you can continue to get Housing Benefit for up to one year. If you are deemed to be liable for the Council Tax you can continue to get Council Tax Benefit. Absences from home include things like being admitted to hospital, going to prison, working away from home or going on holiday. If you go into hospital for six weeks or more, your benefits may be reduced. You cannot get benefit if you sublet your home while you are away.

Benefit for two homes

You can normally only get Housing Benefit for one home. However, if you have moved to a new home and payments on both homes are unavoidable, you may get benefit on both for up to four weeks. There are, however, certain specific circumstances when payments are made for two homes, so ask the council whether you qualify.

Council Tax Benefit is only payable for the home in which you are resident. It is not payable for second homes.

Hardship relief

In cases of hardship the council has the discretion to increase the amount of benefit you can receive if your circumstances are 'exceptional'. They could increase the amount of Housing Benefit and Council Tax Benefit you get up to the maximum amounts. You should ask if you think you should be treated as a special case.

How to claim

If you claim Income Support you will be given a claim form NHB 1 to complete along with the Income Support claim form. The staff at the Benefits Agency (social security) office will work out whether you are entitled to Income Support and notify the council, who will calculate your Housing Benefit and Council Tax Benefit. If you are a private tenant, the council will send you a form to complete, asking for details of your accommodation, how much rent you pay, and whether this includes service or heating charges. Only when they have this information can the council work out how much Housing Benefit to pay.

If you are not claiming Income Support, you claim Housing Benefit and Council Tax Benefit directly from your local council.

If you are a couple, only one of you should claim for benefit – it does not matter if the bill is sent in joint names or just to one of you. Your benefit will be calculated on the basis of your combined income and savings.

Before the council can work out how much to pay, they may require evidence such as rent and pension books, bank statements and evidence of your savings. Benefit is normally awarded for a fixed period of up to 60 weeks, and you will receive another claim form to make a fresh claim at the end of this period.

Change of circumstances

You have a duty to tell the council about any changes in your income or circumstances. If you fail to do this and they discover later that you have been getting more benefit than you are entitled to, you may be asked to pay it back. Likewise, you may find that you have not been getting enough benefit. If you delay reporting a change in your circumstances, you may lose some arrears.

Overpayment

If you are paid too much benefit this is known as an overpayment and in most circumstances the council can ask you to repay this money. However, an overpayment cannot normally be recovered if it was caused by an 'official error' and you could not reasonably be expected to have known you were being overpaid at the time. Even if the council can recover the benefit they do have some discretion about whether to do so. It may be a good idea to seek further advice if you are being asked to repay benefit.

Backdating

The council can backdate your claim for benefit for up to 52 weeks. You must show that you have a good reason for claiming late – for example you have been ill, or there has been a family crisis.

If the council delays your claim

The council should let you know within 14 days of your claim whether you qualify for help. However, this sometimes takes much longer. If you should suffer hardship because the council has not yet worked out your claim for benefit, contact your nearest Citizens Advice Bureau or advice centre for help. If pressure from them cannot speed up the assessment, it may be necessary to ask a local councillor to refer your complaint to the Local Government Ombudsman, who investigates maladministration.

How it is paid

For council tenants, Housing Benefit is usually paid by reducing the rent. Private or housing association tenants can choose to have Housing Benefit paid into a bank account or to the landlord, or to receive a giro cheque.

Most people will pay the Council Tax directly to their local council, so when you claim benefit your bill will be reduced accordingly. Where this is not possible because, for example, you have already paid the whole bill, the council may send you a refund.

Is your benefit the wrong amount?

You can write to the council at any time, asking for further information about how decisions about your benefit have been made. You can ask for a review of a decision relating to your benefit, perhaps because you think you have been awarded the wrong amount.

You should write to the council explaining why you would like the decision reviewed. You should do this within six weeks of receiving the decision, although the council may extend this time limit if there are good reasons for you not writing sooner. The council will then write to you either altering or confirming the decision.

Appealing to a review board

If you still disagree with a decision, you can ask for a further review; but you must ask for it in writing within 28 days of the decision on the first review giving the reasons why you think the council's decision is wrong. Your case will then go to a review board, which consists of at least three local councillors. You can attend the hearing and put your case or a representative can do this on your behalf. The board's decision must normally be sent to you within 14 days, with the reasons for the decision.

If you appeal to a review board, get advice from a Citizens Advice Bureau, welfare rights advice centre or independent housing advice centre. They may find someone who can represent you at the hearing.

Benefits for People with Disabilities and Their Carers

This part of Your Rights *describes the main benefits available to people with disabilities and those who look after them.*

Disability Living Allowance and Attendance Allowance are intended to cover the extra costs associated with disability while other benefits such as Invalidity Benefit and Severe Disablement Allowance are paid to people who are unable to work or can only work to a limited extent because of their disability.

ATTENDANCE ALLOWANCE AND DISABILITY LIVING ALLOWANCE (NOT TAXABLE)

Attendance Allowance and Disability Living Allowance are intended to help with the costs of being disabled. Attendance Allowance is for people who become disabled after the age of 65 or who become disabled at a younger age but only make a claim after they reach 66. If you were disabled before the age of 65 and have not yet reached 66, you should apply for Disability Living Allowance (DLA) instead. This section covers first the conditions for Attendance Allowance and then the conditions for Disability Living Allowance; the third part gives information that applies to both allowances.

Attendance Allowance

This is a benefit for people with severe disabilities, either physical or mental, who need help with personal care, supervision, or to have someone watching over them. It does not depend on NI contributions, is not affected by savings or income, and will not normally affect other benefits or pensions received.

However, Attendance Allowance is normally counted as income if you are receiving Income Support in a residential or nursing home, as explained on pages 106–107.

There are two weekly rates:

Higher rate   £44.90
Lower rate   £30.00

Who qualifies for Attendance Allowance?

To qualify for Attendance Allowance you must fulfil the following conditions:

- You are aged 65 or older (but if you are not yet 66 and you became disabled before the age of 65 you should claim

Disability Living Allowance instead). There is no upper age limit for Attendance Allowance.

- You meet the day and/or night conditions described below.
- You must also normally have met the day and/or night conditions for at least six months, but there are 'special rules' for people who are terminally ill, as explained on pages 79–80.
- You are normally resident in the United Kingdom when you make your claim, and (unless you are applying under the special rules for terminally ill people) have been here for at least 26 weeks of the last 12 months.

You will receive the lower rate if you fulfil either the day or the night conditions. You will get the higher rate if you fulfil both day and night conditions.

You can receive the allowance if you live alone or with other people and regardless of whether or not you receive any help from someone else – what matters is that you need help with personal care, supervision or watching over, not whether you are actually getting it. You do not have to spend the allowance on buying care: it is up to you how you use it. However, your local authority may take it into account when assessing whether, and how much, you need to pay for any social services you have.

Day conditions

You can get the allowance if you are so disabled that you require frequent help throughout the day with your normal 'bodily functions' such as eating, getting up or down stairs, going to the toilet or washing. You can also get the allowance if you need continual supervision throughout the day to avoid putting yourself or others in substantial danger.

Night conditions

You can get the allowance if you are so disabled that you require prolonged (periods of at least 20 minutes) or repeated (at least twice nightly) attention during the night to help you with your bodily functions – for example, going to the toilet and getting in and out of bed. You can also get the allowance if another person needs to be awake for a prolonged period or at frequent intervals throughout the night in order to watch over you to avoid putting yourself or others in substantial danger.

The next section covers the qualifying conditions for Disability Living Allowance, so you should turn to pages 77–82 for information that covers both allowances such as how to make a claim and what happens if you are away from home.

Disability Living Allowance

This benefit has replaced Attendance Allowance and Mobility Allowance for people who become disabled before the age of 65. It is for disabled people who:

- need help with personal care, supervision, or to have someone watching over them *or*
- are unable to walk, have great difficulty walking, or need someone with them when walking outdoors *or*
- need help with both of these.

Disability Living Allowance (DLA) does not depend on NI contributions, is not affected by savings or income, and will not normally affect other benefits or pensions received. However, the care component of DLA is normally counted as income if you are receiving Income Support in a residential or nursing home, as explained on pages 106–107.

There are two parts to DLA: the 'care component', which is paid at one of three rates, and the 'mobility component', which has two different levels. These are the weekly rates:

DLA care component		DLA mobility component	
Higher rate	£44.90	Higher rate	£31.40
Middle rate	£30.00	Lower rate	£11.95
Lower rate	£11.95		

Who qualifies for DLA?

To qualify for DLA you must fulfil the following conditions:

- You meet one or more of the care or mobility conditions described below.

- You are aged under 65 or you became disabled before you reached 65 and you have not yet had your 66th birthday (otherwise you should claim Attendance Allowance instead).

- You must also normally have fulfilled the day and/or night conditions for at least three months, and be expected to qualify for at least the next six months, but there are 'special rules' for people who are terminally ill, as explained on pages 79–80.

- You are normally resident in the United Kingdom when you make your claim, and (unless you are applying under the special rules for terminally ill people) have been here for at least 26 weeks of the last 12 months.

Although you must have become disabled before the age of 65 and have made an application before your 66th birthday, once you are awarded the allowance it will continue, without an age limit, as long as you fulfil either care or mobility conditions.

The care component

The care component of DLA is for people who need help with personal care, supervision or watching over because of physical or mental disabilities. It does not matter if you live alone or with other people, or whether or not you receive any help from someone else – what matters is that you need help with personal care, supervision or watching over, not whether you are actually getting help. You do not have to spend the allowance on paying for care: it is up to you how you use it. However, your local authority may take it into account when assessing whether, and how much, you need to pay for any social services you have.

You will receive the £11.95 rate if you fulfil the lower rate conditions but not the day or night conditions described below. You will receive the middle level if you fulfil either the day or the night conditions while the higher level is for those who fulfil both day and night conditions. You will see that the day and night conditions are the same as those for Attendance Allowance.

Lower rate conditions
You will fulfil this condition if you need help with 'bodily functions' for a significant portion of the day, either at one single period or a number of times. For example, you might need some help to get up in the morning and go to bed in the evening but manage alone for the rest of the day. You will also fulfil this condition if you could not prepare a main cooked meal for yourself even if you had the ingredients.

Day conditions
You will fulfil this condition if you are so disabled that you require frequent help throughout the day with your normal bodily functions such as eating, getting up or down stairs, going to the toilet or washing. You can also get the allowance if you need continual supervision throughout the day to avoid putting yourself or others in substantial danger.

Night conditions
You will fulfil this condition if you are so disabled that you require prolonged (periods of at least 20 minutes) or repeated (at least twice nightly) attention during the night to help you with your bodily functions – for example, going to the toilet and getting in and out of bed. You can also get the allowance if another person needs to be awake for a prolonged period or at frequent intervals throughout the night in order to watch over you to avoid putting yourself or others in substantial danger.

The mobility component

Although the mobility component is given to people who need help getting around, you can spend it how you choose. Remember it is not available to people who become disabled after the age of 65.

You will receive the higher level if you are unable to walk or have great difficulty in walking because of a physical disability. The higher level is also available to people who are both blind and deaf and need someone with them when outdoors, to all people who have lost both legs at or above the ankle, and to certain severely mentally disabled people who have behavioural problems. If you can walk but need someone with you for guidance or supervision, you may be awarded the lower level.

Using a car
If you own a car and get the higher mobility component of DLA, you may not have to pay road tax. If someone drives a car for you, they can also apply for exemption from road tax. You will get details about this and about getting a car through the Motability Scheme when you first get the allowance.

You can also apply to the local authority for an orange badge which allows parking with some limitations but without charge at meters or where waiting is restricted. Some local authorities make a small charge for issuing the orange badge.

Examples of people who may receive DLA

Ellen is 62 and cannot walk very far due to severe arthritis. Although she can manage to care for herself she finds cooking very difficult because she cannot do tasks such as cutting, lifting and pouring. She applied for DLA and was awarded the higher level of the mobility component and the lowest level of the care component.

Albert is 64 and suffers from dementia. During the day his wife or another relative stays with him all the time because he is very forgetful and sometimes wanders off or turns on the gas without lighting it. He normally sleeps all through the night.

His wife applied for DLA on his behalf and he was awarded the middle level of the care component (because he needs supervision during the day) and the lower level of the mobility component because he needs guidance when outdoors.

Sarah is 68 and had a severe stroke six months ago which left her unable to walk and needing a lot of help, for example with washing, dressing and eating. Because she is 68 she is too old to claim DLA. She cannot get any help with her mobility needs but she can apply for Attendance Allowance because she needs personal care.

Remember these are just examples and your situation is probably different. Whether you qualify for DLA, and if so at what level, will depend on your particular circumstances.

Rules covering both Attendance Allowance and Disability Living Allowance

If you are away from home

If you are receiving NHS treatment in a hospital you cannot start to receive Attendance Allowance or the care component of DLA. However, you may receive either of these allowances if you are a private patient paying for the cost of hospital services.

If you are already receiving Attendance Allowance or the care component of DLA and you go into hospital you will be able to continue to receive the allowance for up to four weeks. However, the allowance will stop sooner if your admission is within 28 days of a previous stay in hospital. Normally you can apply for, or continue to receive, the mobility component of DLA if you are in hospital.

For information about Attendance Allowance and DLA for people in residential or nursing homes see pages 106–107. In general, a holiday abroad does not affect Attendance

Allowance or DLA, nor do periods abroad for medical treatment. You should let your Benefits Agency (social security) office know when you intend to go abroad so that payment of the allowance while you are abroad can be considered.

How to claim

The claim packs for Attendance Allowance and DLA are quite long; the intention is that people can describe how their disability affects them. This means a medical examination will not normally be necessary. Do not be put off by the length of the form. If you have difficulties filling it in then a friend or relative can fill in the form for you, a local advice agency may be able to help, or you can telephone the Benefits Enquiry Line for advice – the number is on the claim form. If it is difficult for you to get out your local Benefits Agency (social security) office may be able to arrange for a visiting officer to call to help you with the form.

There are two sections of the form: one deals with information about yourself and the second asks about how your disability or illness affects you. If you have difficulty with the second section or would rather have a medical examination then you can ask for a doctor to visit.

The second section of the form asks about the sort of help you need. Remember that it does not matter if you actually receive any help or not. Be sure to say what activities are difficult or impossible for you to do. For example, you may have to get dressed on your own because there is no one to help you but do explain if it takes a long time or if it is difficult – perhaps because you get out of breath. If you feel that having answered the questions you have not given a good picture of how your disability affects you, add any extra information you think would be helpful. If you have any problems with filling in the form, do ask for help. There is also a space on the form for your doctor or someone else who knows about your circumstances to complete.

If your claim cannot be decided from the information in the form the Benefits Agency may ask for further information from someone such as your doctor or district nurse or they may arrange a medical examination. If an appointment is made for a doctor to visit, you may want a friend or relative to be there at that time. This will be particularly important if you have difficulty making yourself understood. The doctor, who will not be your own doctor but one appointed by the DSS, will probably examine you and ask further questions. It may be useful to make a note beforehand of the things you need to tell the doctor about when you need help or the difficulties you experience.

You can get the claim pack for Attendance Allowance or DLA from the local Benefits Agency (social security) office, or by telephoning the Benefits Enquiry Line on 0800 882 200 or by sending off the tear-off slip on leaflet DS 702 (Attendance Allowance) or DS 704 (DLA). You should return the form in the envelope provided within six weeks or you may lose some benefit.

When to claim

Although you normally need to fulfil the qualifying conditions for three months before you can start getting DLA and six months for Attendance Allowance, if you have only recently become disabled you should still apply as it may take some weeks to deal with your claim. If you are receiving a lower level of one of the allowances but your condition has deteriorated so you might now qualify for a higher level, you can ask for your case to be reviewed. You will need to qualify for the higher level for three months (DLA) or six months (Attendance Allowance) before it can be paid.

Terminal illness

People who are terminally ill can claim Attendance Allowance or DLA without the three-month or six-month waiting period. They will be considered to be terminally ill if their illness is expected to limit their life expectancy to six months or less.

To claim ask your doctor for a DS 1500 report, which gives details of your condition. Send this in the envelope provided along with section 1 of the Attendance Allowance or DLA form. You do not need to complete the part which covers 'Help with personal care': if you are assessed as being terminally ill, you will automatically receive the higher rate of Attendance Allowance or the highest level of the care component of DLA. However, if you are under 66 and want to claim the mobility part of DLA you will need to fill in the section on 'Help with getting around' and include this with your claim. Claims should be dealt with within 10–14 days and a medical examination will not normally be necessary.

An application can be made by another person on behalf of someone who is terminally ill, so it is possible for people to receive an allowance under the special rules without knowing their diagnosis.

How it is paid

Attendance Allowance or DLA may be awarded indefinitely or for a set period, in which case it will be reviewed at the end of this time. Attendance Allowance is either paid by weekly order book or paid four-weekly in arrears directly into a bank or building society account. If you are receiving another benefit or pension they will normally be paid together. DLA is normally paid four-weekly unless you were getting Attendance Allowance by weekly order book before April 1992. However, people claiming under the special rules because they are terminally ill can get weekly payments.

Is the allowance the wrong amount?

If you are refused an allowance or awarded a lower rate than you expected, you can ask for your case to be reviewed. You should ask for a review within three months of receiving the original decision. You should send in any additional written information that might help. A different adjudication officer will look at your case and may ask for extra evidence from people who know you such as your own doctor.

If you are not satisfied with the outcome of the review then you can appeal against the decision. You should do this within three months of receiving the review decision. Your case will then go to a Social Security Appeal Tribunal if you are appealing against a non-medical decision such as whether you fulfil the residency conditions, or a Disability Appeal Tribunal if you disagree with a decision about whether you fulfil the attendance, supervision or mobility conditions. The Disability Appeal Tribunal will consist of three people not connected with the DSS, at least one of whom should be experienced in dealing with the needs of disabled people. At the tribunal you or a representative will be able to put your case as to why the decision should be changed.

If you want a review or appeal, you may find it useful to seek help locally and read the *Disability Rights Handbook* (see p 126 for details about how to get a copy).

For Attendance Allowance see social security leaflet DS 702 and claim pack DS 2. For DLA see social security leaflet DS 704 and claim pack DLA 1.

INVALID CARE ALLOWANCE
(TAXABLE)

This is a benefit for people who are unable to work full-time because they are caring for a severely disabled person for at least 35 hours a week. The benefit is not dependent on having paid NI contributions.

The weekly rates are shown below:

Carer   £33.70

Adult dependant   £20.15

The person being cared for must be receiving one of the allowances referred to below such as Attendance Allowance. He or she does not have to be a relative and may live separately or with the carer.

Who qualifies?

As a carer, you can claim the allowance whether you are married or single provided you spend at least 35 hours a week looking after someone who is receiving Attendance Allowance (higher or lower rate), the care component of Disability Living Allowance (middle or higher level), or Constant Attendance Allowance of £36.70 or more paid with an industrial, war or service pension.

You must be over 16 and under 65 when you first claim – women aged 60–64 should read the section below on 'Age limits for men and women'. You must also be resident in the United Kingdom and have lived here for at least 26 weeks out of the past 12 months.

You cannot get Invalid Care Allowance (ICA) if you earn more than £50 a week after the deduction of certain work expenses. The extra £20.15 which can be claimed for a dependent adult will not be paid if that person earns more than £20.15 a week (allowing for reasonable work expenses), including any occupational or personal pension. It also may not be paid if he or she is receiving a State pension or benefit.

Age limits for men and women

At the time of writing, according to British law women must first claim ICA before the age of 60, while men must claim before they reach 65. However, in a test case, the Court of Appeal ruled that under European law the age limit for men and women should be the same. This case has now been heard in the European Court and a ruling is expected around April 1993. In the meantime women aged 60–64 may be able to start receiving ICA if they fulfil the other conditions. However, in some cases women will not be any better off if they are already receiving a Retirement Pension or another benefit. Contact Age Concern England for further information.

Overlap with other benefits

If you are already getting £33.70 a week or more from certain other social security benefits or pensions, you may not be able to get ICA as well. This is because ICA 'overlaps' with some benefits including Invalidity Benefit, Retirement Pension and Widow's Pension.

If you have a spouse or partner who is claiming an addition to his or her benefit for you, that addition will be reduced by the amount of ICA received.

Example

Olive looks after her disabled mother, who gets Attendance Allowance. Olive's husband, Wilfred, is also ill and receives Invalidity Benefit with an addition of £33.70 for Olive. When Olive claims Invalid Care Allowance of £33.70 a week, the benefit that Wilfred gets for her is reduced by the same amount (£33.70). This means that the benefit Wilfred gets for Olive is stopped altogether, although his own Invalidity Benefit continues to be paid.

However, if you have a low income it may still be worth claiming ICA even though it may not be paid in addition to your present benefit or pension. Although ICA is counted as income if you claim Income Support, Housing Benefit or Council Tax Benefit, people entitled to ICA may be able to get higher rates of these benefits, due to the 'carer premium', as explained on pages 44–45.

Protecting your pension

If you receive ICA, NI contributions will be automatically credited to protect your right to a future Retirement Pension unless you have retained the right to pay the married woman's reduced rate contributions. If you receive another benefit instead and are not working regularly because you are caring for someone, you may get Home Responsibilities Protection (see pp 17–19).

When you reach pension age

When you reach pension age (60 for women, 65 for men), ICA will be adjusted to take account of any Retirement Pension you draw. If your pension is more than £33.70, the allowance will stop. If your pension is less than £33.70, the allowance will be reduced by the amount of pension received.

If you are not entitled to a pension or do not claim one, ICA can continue as long as the other rules are satisfied.

If you are still receiving ICA at the age of 65 (women) or 70 (men), it can continue to be paid even though you are no longer caring for a disabled person.

See social security claim pack DS 700. The Carers National Association produces information for carers. Their address is Carers National Association, 29 Chilworth Mews, London W2 3RG.

STATUTORY SICK PAY (TAXABLE) AND SICKNESS BENEFIT (NOT TAXABLE)

If you are an employee paying NI contributions and you are under pension age (60 for women, 65 for men), you will probably be entitled to Statutory Sick Pay (SSP) if you are off sick for at least four days in a row. This can continue for up to 28 weeks. The amount will depend on your level of earnings and it will be paid by your employer. You may also get sick pay from your employer's own scheme depending on your terms and conditions.

If you are unable to work because of sickness but not entitled to SSP, for example because you are self-employed, unemployed or over pension age (and not drawing your State Pension), you may be entitled to Sickness Benefit, depending on your NI contributions. This can be paid for up to 28 weeks.

The full weekly rates for someone under pension age are given below:

Claimant   £42.70

Adult dependant   £26.40

If you are over pension age but have not reached 65 (women) or 70 (men) you can claim Sickness Benefit if you would have been entitled to a State Pension but have not chosen to draw it. If you only have enough contributions for a reduced pension your Sickness Benefit will also be reduced. You can draw the full amount of Sickness Benefit if you are ill due to an industrial accident or an industrial disease. The full weekly rates for people over pension age are given below:

Claimant   £53.80

Adult dependant   £32.30

In addition you will receive any Graduated or Additional Pension you had earned up to pension age. The weeks when you claim Sickness Benefit will not count towards extra pension when you finally claim your pension.

Equal treatment of men and women

Because there are different rates of Sickness Benefit for people above or below pension age you may find you are receiving less benefit than a person of the opposite sex who is the same age as you. In some cases it may be possible to challenge this on the grounds that European law does not allow unequal treatment of men and women. For further information seek local advice or contact Age Concern England.

See social security leaflets NI 244 (Statutory Sick Pay) and NI 16 (Sickness Benefit).

INVALIDITY BENEFIT (NOT TAXABLE)

Invalidity Benefit is paid to people who have been unable to work for at least 28 weeks through illness or disability. It depends on NI contributions, but is not normally affected by savings or other income, although the level of benefit is sometimes reduced when you reach pension age if you have an occupational pension.

The benefit consists of the basic Invalidity Pension and – for some people – an Invalidity Allowance based on age and/or an Additional Pension related to earnings. Invalidity Pension weekly rates are shown below:

Claimant	£56.10
Adult dependant	£33.70

The Invalidity Allowance is an extra amount for people who first become incapable of work more than five years before State Pension age (60 for women, 65 for men – but see the section on 'Equal treatment of men and women' below). There are three rates depending on your age at the time you became unable to work, but you will not receive the full amount if you are entitled to an Additional Invalidity Pension as well. Invalidity Allowance rates are shown below:

Under 40	£11.95
40–49	£7.50
Men 50–59, women 50–54	£3.75

The Additional Invalidity Pension is based on earnings between April 1978 and April 1991 and is worked out in the same way as the Additional Retirement Pension (see pp 21–23). It is paid even if your occupational scheme was contracted out of SERPS but may be reduced when you reach pension age, as described below. However, earnings after April 1991 will not count towards an Additional Pension paid with Invalidity Benefit.

■ You cannot get both the Additional Invalidity Pension and the maximum Invalidity Allowance. If your Additional Pension is higher than the Invalidity Allowance, you will not receive any Invalidity Allowance. If your Additional Pension is less, it will be topped up to the level of the Invalidity Allowance.

Example
Ashton became too ill to work at 45 and is entitled to Invalidity Allowance of £7.50 a week. However, because he is entitled to £5 a week Additional Pension, he only gets £2.50 Invalidity Allowance to give him a total of £7.50 a week (on top of the Invalidity Pension of £56.10).

Who qualifies?

To get Invalidity Benefit, you must have been entitled to Sickness Benefit and have been receiving it or Statutory Sick Pay (SSP) for 28 weeks. If you do not qualify for Invalidity Benefit because you were not entitled to Sickness Benefit, you may get Severe Disablement Allowance (see pp 90–91).

Increases for a husband or wife

You can claim the adult dependant increase for your spouse if he or she does not earn more than £44.65 a week. (Any occupational or personal pension received is counted as earnings.) If your spouse is receiving another benefit, you may not get all or any of the addition for him or her. These increases are similar to the increases for dependants paid with the Retirement Pension. See page 11 for more information.

Work and Invalidity Benefit

You cannot get Invalidity Benefit if you work unless it is of a 'therapeutic' nature, undertaken on the advice of your doctor and approved by the Benefits Agency (social security) office. The maximum you can earn is £42 a week after allowable expenses.

When you reach pension age

When you reach pension age (60 for women, 65 for men), you can draw the Retirement Pension or continue claiming Invalidity Benefit up to the age of 65 (women) or 70 (men).

You cannot continue to receive Invalidity Benefit after the age of 65 (women) or 70 (men), so at that time you should draw the Retirement Pension. If it appears that you are worse off than someone of your age of the opposite sex, read the section on 'Equal treatment of men and women' below.

Drawing your pension

If you draw the Retirement Pension at pension age, instead of continuing to claim Invalidity Benefit, it will be worked out according to the normal rules. Depending on your contributions this may include Basic Pension, Additional Pension (adjusted for any periods when you were contracted out of SERPS) and Graduated Pension. In addition you will continue to receive any Invalidity Allowance which you were receiving before reaching pension age.

Invalidity Benefit after pension age

If you do not draw the State Pension at 60 (women) or 65 (men), you can continue to get Invalidity Pension while you remain incapable of work, provided you would qualify for the State Pension. However, any day for which you are paid Invalidity Pension will not count towards extra pension when you finally claim your pension.

When you reach pension age, Invalidity Pension will be paid at the maximum rate of £56.10 a week only if your Retirement Pension would have been payable at the full basic rate, or if your inability to work resulted from an industrial accident or an industrial disease. If you are only entitled to a reduced Retirement Pension, your Invalidity Pension will also be reduced.

In addition to the basic Invalidity Pension, you will also receive any Graduated Pension to which you are entitled, and any Invalidity Allowance you were receiving before you reached pension age.

If you belonged to a contracted-out pension scheme, the amount of Additional Pension paid with your Invalidity Pension will be reduced when you reach pension age. This is because you will be getting a Guaranteed Minimum Pension or your Protected Rights from the scheme, as explained on pages 22–23.

Choosing when to draw your pension

Once you reach pension age Invalidity Benefit will normally be paid at the same or a similar level to the Retirement Pension you could draw. You can ask your local Benefits Agency (social security) office for an estimate of your pension and how much your Invalidity Benefit will be when you reach pension age.

In deciding whether to draw your pension, you should note that at present Invalidity Benefit is not taxable, whereas the State Pension (including Invalidity Allowance paid with it) is taxable. However, there are earnings limits for Invalidity Benefit but not for the State Pension. You may wish to consult a local advice agency if you are unsure which to claim.

Equal treatment of men and women

Because of the different pension ages men and women sometimes receive different amounts of Invalidity Pension. For example, a man disabled at the age of 59 would receive some Invalidity Allowance whereas a woman of the same age would not. At the time of writing this was being challenged as unlawful under European law, which says that for most benefits men and women should be treated equally. If you receive less Invalidity Pension than someone of the opposite sex of the same age, you can appeal against this. For further information contact a local advice agency or Age Concern England.

How to claim

When you first become unable to work, you may receive Statutory Sick Pay (SSP) from your employer or be able to claim Sickness Benefit from your local Benefits Agency (social security) office. After 28 weeks, you will be automatically transferred to Invalidity Benefit if you were getting Sickness Benefit; you will be given a claim form by your employer if you were getting SSP. You will be required to continue sending in sick certificates from the doctor.

Is your benefit the wrong amount?

If you think you have been awarded the wrong amount of Invalidity Benefit or disagree with another decision concerning it, you can ask for the case to be reviewed or you can appeal, as explained on pages 33–34.

See social security leaflet NI 16A (Invalidity Benefit).

SEVERE DISABLEMENT ALLOWANCE (NOT TAXABLE)

This is a benefit for people who are unable to work because of long-term disability or sickness and have not paid enough contributions to get Sickness or Invalidity Benefit. The basic weekly rates are shown below:

Claimant	£33.70
Adult dependant	£20.15

There are also additions for people who became unable to work before the age of 60; these are added to the basic rate of £33.70. The weekly rates are shown below:

Under 40	£11.95
40–49	£7.50
50–59	£3.75

Who qualifies?

You must be under 65 (for both men and women) when you first apply and have been unable to work for at least 196 days. Women aged 60–64 should read 'Age limits for men and women' below. You also need to be normally resident in the United Kingdom and have been living here for at least 26 out of the last 52 weeks. You will have to be assessed as being '80 per cent disabled', or you must be drawing another benefit such as Attendance Allowance or Disability Living Allowance (the higher rate of the mobility component or the middle or higher rate of the care component).

Severe Disablement Allowance (SDA) 'overlaps' with certain other benefits, so if you are already receiving another benefit or pension, you may not get both. If your husband or wife is receiving an addition for you with his or her pension or benefit, then this may be stopped or reduced if you are awarded SDA.

You cannot receive both the full amount of SDA and a Retirement Pension. If you do not qualify for a Retirement Pension or it is less than SDA, you can continue to receive SDA to make your benefit up to the basic level of £33.70 plus the age addition if you qualify for one. Instead of drawing your pension, you can also continue to receive the allowance.

Age limits for men and women

At the time of writing, according to British law women must first claim SDA before the age of 60, while men must claim before they reach 65. However, in a test case, the Court of Appeal ruled that under European law the age limit for men and women should be the same. This case has now been heard in the European Court and a ruling is expected around April 1993. In the meantime women aged 60–64 may be able to start receiving SDA if they fulfil the other conditions. However, in some cases women will not be any better off if they are already receiving a Retirement Pension or another benefit. Contact Age Concern England for further information.

See social security leaflet NI 252.

OTHER BENEFITS FOR PEOPLE WITH DISABILITIES

This section gives brief information about other benefits for people with disabilities. More detailed information is given in the leaflets mentioned or you could look at the *Disability Rights Handbook* (see p 126 for details).

Disability Working Allowance (DWA)

This allowance started in April 1992 and is a benefit for disabled people who are employed but are only able to earn low wages. To qualify you will need to work for at least 16 hours a week, have recently been receiving one or more of certain disability benefits including Invalidity Benefit and Severe Disablement Allowance, have a disability which puts you 'at a disadvantage in getting a job', and have no more than £16,000 in savings. If you fulfil these conditions, whether you receive DWA, and if so how much you can get, will depend on your income and savings and factors such as the people in your family.

If you give up a benefit such as Invalidity Benefit in order to work and draw DWA but stop working within two years, you will be able to start drawing your previous benefit again as long as you still fulfil the incapacity conditions.

If you are considering giving up your disability benefit in order to work and claim DWA, it is a good idea to seek advice first from a local agency. In some cases claiming DWA may not be the best thing for you to do – for example, you might be better off staying on Invalidity Benefit and undertaking 'therapeutic' work, for which you could earn up to £42.

See social security leaflet DS 703 and claim pack including form DWA 1.

Industrial injuries scheme

The industrial injuries scheme can provide help to people who are disabled as a result of an accident at work or an industrial disease. The main benefit is Disablement Benefit, which can be paid in addition to any other national insurance benefits such as Invalidity Benefit, Sickness Benefit or Retirement Pension. The level of payment depends on how disabled you are assessed as being. If you are awarded Disablement Benefit at the 100 per cent rate, you may also qualify for Constant Attendance Allowance if you need care and attention. There is also an Exceptionally Severe Disablement Allowance for those who are likely to need high levels of attention on a permanent basis.

See social security leaflets NI 2 (industrial diseases) and NI 6 (Disablement Benefit).

War pensions and war widows' pensions

You may be entitled to a War Disablement Pension if you were disabled as a result of service in the armed forces between 4 August 1914 and 30 September 1921 or at any time since 2 September 1939. The amount awarded depends on how disabled you are. Civilians disabled by a war injury may also qualify for a War Disablement Pension. There are extra allowances which may be paid in addition to a War Disablement Pension. These include a Constant Attendance Allowance for people needing a lot of care and attention and a Mobility Supplement if you have difficulty walking because of your disability.

You may be entitled to a War Widow's Pension if you are the widow of someone whose death was due to service in the armed forces or to a war injury. The amount paid depends on the rank of the person who has died and the age of the widow.

The War Pensioners' Welfare Service has welfare officers who can offer help and advice to war pensioners and war widows who have problems about pensions or other matters. If you wish to consult a welfare officer you should contact your nearest War Pensioners' Welfare Office. Your local Benefits Agency (social security) office will give you the address or you will find it in either of the leaflets mentioned below.

See social security leaflets MPL 153 (war disabled) and MPL 152 (war widows).

INDEPENDENT LIVING FUND

The Independent Living Fund provided cash payments to help severely disabled people who needed to pay for personal care or household tasks in order to remain living at home. It was only intended to run for five years and it stopped taking new applications in November 1992.

Two new funds have replaced the Independent Living Fund. The first, the Independent Living (Extension) Fund, will continue to provide assistance to those receiving Independent Living Fund payments on 31 March 1993, although the help given may be reviewed.

The Independent Living (1993) Fund can accept new applications but its scope is more limited than the previous Independent Living Fund. Full details are not available at the time of writing, but the new Fund is intended to help severely disabled people aged 16–65 for whom the costs of care at home would be more than the cost of a place in a residential or nursing home. The needs of the disabled person will be assessed and agreed by the local authority, social workers from the new fund and the disabled person themselves.

Contact your local authority or Age Concern England for further information.

Other Financial Benefits

This part of Your Rights *gives details about other financial help that may be available for older people. It covers a variety of subjects including paying for fuel, health costs, Legal Aid, and help towards the fees for residential and nursing home care.*

Most, but not all, of the financial assistance outlined depends on your income and savings or whether you are receiving another benefit such as Income Support or Housing Benefit.

If you live in Scotland you should note the position is different regarding help with legal costs and grants for repairs and improvements. Contact Age Concern Scotland (address on p 127) for more information.

PAYING FOR FUEL, INSULATION AND REPAIRS

The cost of fuel is a major expense for most pensioners. This section outlines what help is available and the different ways to pay your bills.

Fuel debts

If you cannot pay your fuel bills, you may be threatened with disconnection. However, British Gas and the electricity companies publish Codes of Practice which state that if everyone in the household who has an income is a pensioner, the fuel supply should not be disconnected between 1 October and 31 March. They must also follow set procedures before they can disconnect someone – for example, they must first offer payment options or the installation of a prepayment meter. You should check that the fuel board is aware that you are a pensioner and also seek advice about making payments, as described below. The protection against disconnection will not apply if it is clear you can afford to pay a bill but have not done so.

As soon as you realise that you cannot pay a fuel bill, you should contact the fuel board concerned. Do not delay, as it will be much easier to sort out any problems before debts mount up. You can arrange with British Gas or the electricity company to pay a bill in instalments or have a prepayment meter installed. If possible you should also contact a Citizens Advice Bureau or a local Age Concern group for help in making arrangements with the fuel boards and to ensure that you can afford the agreed repayments.

'Fuel direct'

If you have a fuel debt and are receiving Income Support, you may be able to avoid disconnection or get reconnected by going on 'fuel direct'. Some of your benefit will be withheld every week and paid directly to the fuel board to cover the cost of fuel being used and the amount owed. If you think that too large an amount is being withheld, ask the local Benefits Agency (social security) office which administers your Income Support whether the fuel board will accept a smaller amount.

Cold Weather Payments

If you are receiving one of the pensioner or disability premiums with Income Support, you will receive a Cold Weather Payment, currently £6 a week, for each period of seven consecutive days when the average temperature in your area has been, or is expected to be, 0° Celsius or below. These payments will be made automatically so you do not have to make a claim.

See social security leaflet CWP 1.

Paying your bills

Most electricity and gas customers receive their fuel before paying for it (ie on credit), with the amount used recorded by a 'credit meter'. Customers are sent their bills at the end of each quarter. If you find it hard to pay your bills quarterly, it may be easier to put aside some money regularly by putting it in a building society or post office savings account to earn some interest. Alternatively you can pay by a range of different methods, as outlined below.

Fuel stamps

These can be bought at electricity or gas showrooms and some sub-post offices, and stuck on a card. The stamps are interchangeable so that you can pay a gas bill with electricity stamps and an electricity bill with gas stamps. You cannot exchange these stamps for cash.

Regular payments

British Gas or the electricity company will estimate how much gas or electricity you will use over the next year so that you can make regular payments. The schemes available include paying by direct debit from your bank account, either quarterly or monthly, and a range of flexible payment and budget schemes which allow you to pay weekly, fortnightly or monthly.

At the end of the year, if you have paid too much, either you will get a refund or the amount overpaid will be credited to your account. If you have not paid enough, and the amount owed is small, it may be carried forward to the next year's payments. Otherwise, you will have to pay the difference.

Prepayment meters

The fuel board may install a meter so you can pay for fuel as you use it. Coinless prepayment meters may be operated by tokens, keys or cards which can be bought from showrooms, post offices or 24-hour vending machines in £1 or £5 units. Coin-operated prepayment meters are operated by putting coins into a slot – but these are being replaced by coinless meters. Paying for fuel 'as you go' can be useful as a budgeting aid if you are on a low income as it allows you to regulate your use of fuel. Prepayment meters can also be reset by the fuel supplier to pay off debt. If you are asked to pay for all or part of the cost of installing a prepayment meter and are receiving Income Support, you may be able to get a loan or grant from the Social Fund for the installation charges (see pp 51–54 for more about the Social Fund).

Fuel paid for by prepayment meter may be more expensive than if you receive your fuel on credit. If you pay your landlord for gas and electricity with a prepayment meter, make sure that you are not paying too much. The Citizens Advice Bureau should be able to advise you on this.

See Age Concern England Factsheet 1 *Help with Heating*.

Grants for insulation and draughtproofing

If you receive Income Support, Housing Benefit, Council Tax Benefit or Disability Working Allowance you can get a grant under the Home Energy Efficiency Scheme. These grants are available for loft, pipe, and hot and cold water tank insulation, draughtproofing and basic energy advice. If you do not have loft insulation or the existing material is less than 50mm (2in) thick, you can get a grant to insulate it with material up to 150mm (6in) thick. You can do the work yourself, use a 'network installer', such as a local energy project, or get the work carried out by a contractor. For more information about the scheme and details of local network installers contact Energy Action Grants Agency (address and telephone number on p 125).

The size of the grant will depend on the work you have done, and who does it. At the time of writing (March 1993) the maximum grant is £289, and you will have to pay a contribution up to a maximum of £16 towards this.

The council can also provide 'minor works grants' for basic insulation measures, as explained under 'Help with repairs and improvements'. These grants are 'discretionary' – which means it is up to the council to decide whether or not to give you the help.

Help with repairs and improvements

Home-owners and some private tenants may be able to get a 'renovation grant' towards the cost of certain repairs or improvements from their local council.

These grants will depend on your income and savings. If you qualify on income grounds, some grants are mandatory (which means the council must give them), for example, to install an inside toilet or a hot and cold water supply. Other grants – such as one for reroofing – are discretionary, so they may not always be available.

'Minor works grants', which are also discretionary, are intended to cover smaller items of work such as rewiring and insulating your home, again depending on income and savings. These grants are available to owner-occupiers, private tenants or housing association tenants. To qualify you must receive Income Support, Housing Benefit or Council Tax Benefit.

'Disabled facilities grants' cover a variety of improvement and adaptation work intended to make life easier for someone with a disability. Some are mandatory and some discretionary, depending on the type of work needed. They are also subject to an assessment of income and savings.

If you need help with repairs or improvements, you should apply to the renovation grant section of your local council. You should not start the work or buy any of the materials until you have received the council's approval to go ahead.

In some areas there are special agencies such as 'Care and Repair' or 'Staying Put' projects which give advice and practical assistance to home-owners needing to repair their homes. Your local council or Age Concern group should know whether there is a scheme in your area.

See Age Concern England Factsheet 13 *Older Home-Owners – Financial help with repairs.*

PAYING FOR RESIDENTIAL AND NURSING HOME CARE

This section summarises the help you can get with residential or nursing home charges. There are now different systems of financial support depending on whether someone entered a home before or after 1 April 1993. The first part of this section covers the position for someone who was living in a private or voluntary residential or nursing home before 1 April 1993. The next part looks at the rules for people entering a private, voluntary or local authority home on or after 1 April 1993. This is followed by information for people who were already living in a local authority home when the rules changed. There are then details about when Attendance Allowance, Disability Living Allowance and Housing Benefit can be paid.

People living permanently in private or voluntary residential or nursing homes on 31 March 1993

If you were already resident in a private or voluntary residential or nursing home on 31 March 1993, you are covered by 'preserved entitlement' to the special higher levels of Income Support to help pay the fees. You may already be claiming Income Support if you have savings of £8,000 or less. If you are paying the full fees yourself, you will be eligible to claim Income Support when your savings are reduced to £8,000 or less. You should contact your local Benefits Agency (social security) office about claiming.

If, however, you are living in a home in England or Wales which caters for fewer than four people and you are meeting the full fees yourself, you will not have preserved entitlement to the special higher levels of Income Support. If you need help to meet the home's fees at some time in the future, you will need to go to your local authority.

The amount of Income Support you receive will depend on your income and savings, the type of home you are in and the level of fees charged. Savings between £3,000 and £8,000 will be counted as extra income of £1 a week for every £250 (or part of £250) over £3,000, as explained on page 39 – this is called 'tariff income'.

Income Support will bring your income up to the amount of the fees, subject to a national limit, which is generally £185 a week for residential homes and £280 a week for nursing homes. If the home is in Greater London the limits will be increased by £25 a week for residential homes and £35 a week for nursing homes. There are higher limits for people whose physical disability began before they reached pension age (60 for women, 65 for men), and there is a higher maximum amount for someone in residential care who is blind or who qualifies for the higher rate of Attendance Allowance or the higher level of the care component of Disability Living Allowance (see pp 71–80 for more details about these allowances). An additional £12.65 is also payable for personal expenses.

If the charges for a residential or nursing home are higher than the maximum amount that you can get from Income Support, the difference can be made up from your own savings, or from other sources (eg relatives, friends, charitable assistance) without this affecting your benefit.

Example
Mrs Black lives in a residential home outside London where the charges are £185 per week. She entered the home in 1991 and was paying the fees from the money she received from selling her house. However, her savings are now down to £8,000 so she claims Income Support. Each week she receives a State Pension of £56.10 and an occupational pension of £30. Her Income Support is worked out as follows:

State Pension	£56.10
Occupational pension	£30.00
Tariff income from £8,000 savings	£20.00
Income Support towards fees	£78.90
total	£185.00

In addition Mrs Black will receive £12.65 for personal expenses. If the fees go up by £10 she will not get any extra Income Support because her income is already being brought up to the maximum level allowed. She will have to use her savings or the amount received for personal expenses; or she will have to get help from friends, family or a charity or find a less expensive residential home.

Owning your home

If you own your own home its value will normally be taken into account when your savings are assessed for Income Support.

However, this value will be ignored for 26 weeks, or longer if reasonable, if you are taking steps to sell it. The value of your home will also be ignored if your partner or a 'relative' who is disabled or aged 60 or over lives there. (For details about who counts as a relative in this situation and further information about the treatment of a former home, contact Age Concern England.)

For more detailed information about the system of 'preserved entitlement' to Income Support, see Age Concern England Factsheet 11 *Preserved Entitlement to Income Support for Residential and Nursing Homes* and social security leaflet IS 50.

People applying for a place in a residential or nursing home from 1 April 1993

Private and voluntary homes

If you wish to enter a private or voluntary residential or nursing home from 1 April 1993 and you need help to pay the fees, you will need to be assessed by the local authority (the county, or metropolitan or London borough). The social services department will be responsible for arranging an assessment of your care needs. After this assessment, they will decide whether they can offer you help – either in your own home, or in a residential or nursing home. Each local authority will have its own criteria for making these decisions. If you do not agree with its decision, you can make a complaint through the complaints procedure.

If the local authority agrees to arrange a place for you in a private or voluntary residential or nursing home, it will be responsible for paying the full fee to the home. If you wish, you will be able to choose a different home (subject to certain conditions), but if the home you choose is too expensive, you will have to make arrangements to raise the additional money (for instance, from friends or relatives, or a charity).

The local authority charging procedure will be carried out according to national rules which will be similar but not identical to the Income Support assessment rules. If you have more than £8,000 in savings, you will pay the full fee until your savings reach £8,000. If your savings are £8,000 or less, the local authority will first check to see that you are receiving all the State benefits to which you are entitled. You will be able to claim ordinary Income Support (see pp 38–50) and Residential Allowance, which will be paid as part of Income Support to help with the housing costs of care in residential and nursing homes. This allowance will be £45 per week for homes anywhere in the country except London, where it will be £50 per week. There is also an allowance of £12.65 for personal expenses.

Local authority homes

If you live in a home run by the local authority, you will not be able to claim ordinary Income Support or Residential Allowance. If your income is *less than* the Basic Pension and your savings are not more than £8,000, you may be entitled to Income Support to bring your total income up to the Basic Pension level. From this you would pay the local authority £43.45 per week, leaving you with £12.65 for personal expenses. If your income is *more than* the Basic Pension you will have to pay more towards the fees, although you will still normally be left with at least £12.65.

Owning your home

In you are in a local authority home or the local authority has arranged a place in a private or voluntary home and you own your own home, its value will normally be taken into account, unless your stay is only temporary, or your partner or a 'relative' who is disabled or aged 60 or over lives there. However, the local authority can choose to ignore the value of your home if someone else lives there, for instance a friend aged over 60, or a relative or friend under 60 who has been caring for you for a substantial period.

If the local authority does not ignore the value of your former home it will be able to place a 'charge' on its value, so that it can reclaim money owed to it when the property is sold. You should seek legal advice about this.

The local authority will also be able to take account of certain assets which you might have transferred to someone else in order to pay less for your care. It may be able to recover any debt from the recipients of such assets if the transfer was made within six months of admission to the home.

Local authority homes before 1 April 1993

If you were already living in a local authority home before 1 April 1993, the contribution you have to pay will be reassessed on 12 April 1993. Your income and savings will be assessed in the same way as described above for someone entering a home after April 1993. If you will be worse off under the new system, increased payments will be phased in over three years. In the first year, you should not have to pay any more than you would have been assessed to pay under the old local authority system.

For details about the system for people in local authority homes or needing local authority support in private or voluntary homes after 1 April 1993, see Age Concern England Factsheet 10 *Local Authority Charging Procedures for Residential and Nursing Home Care.*

Attendance Allowance or Disability Living Allowance in a care home

The mobility component of Disability Living Allowance (DLA), which has replaced Mobility Allowance, can normally be claimed and continue to be paid if you are in a local authority home or a private or voluntary home regardless of whether you entered the home before or after 1 April 1993.

Whether or not you receive Attendance Allowance or the care component of DLA will depend on the type of home you are in, when you entered it, and how the fees are being met.

Living in a private or voluntary home on 31 March 1993

If you have been living in a private or voluntary home since before 1 April 1993 and are paying the full charges yourself, then you can claim Attendance Allowance or DLA provided you fulfil the other conditions (see pp 71–73 and 74–76). If you claim Income Support towards payment of a home's fees, Attendance Allowance or the care component of DLA will continue to be paid but will count as income and reduce the amount of Income Support that can be paid.

It may, however, still be beneficial to claim Attendance Allowance or the care component of DLA if you are in a private or voluntary residential home. If you qualify for £44.90 through Attendance Allowance or the higher care component of DLA, or you are blind, the fees will be paid up to a maximum amount of £215 instead of the usual £185 maximum.

Entering a private or voluntary home on or after 1 April 1993

If you are paying the full charges in a private or voluntary home then you can claim Attendance Allowance or DLA provided you fulfil the other conditions (see pp 71–73 and 74–76). You can receive these allowances whether you arranged the admission yourself or the local authority arranged the admission.

However, if you claim Income Support or need local authority financial support in order to meet the home's fees, you cannot start to receive Attendance Allowance or the care component of DLA. If you are already receiving one of these allowances it will stop four weeks after the admission.

Living in a local authority home

If you receive Attendance Allowance or the care component of DLA and you move into a home run by the local authority, the allowance can only continue to be paid for up to four weeks. If you are already living in a local authority home, you cannot start to receive one of these allowances.

Housing Benefit in a care home

Since January 1991 most people in private and voluntary homes have not been able to receive Housing Benefit towards a home's fees. However, people living in such homes and receiving Housing Benefit on 29 October 1990 will be able to continue to receive this provided they are not getting Income Support. This will apply even if they move to a different home or return to a care home after a period in ordinary accommodation.

People may be able to claim Housing Benefit if they live in private or voluntary unregistered homes such as some Abbeyfield homes. Some others will also be able to claim Housing Benefit, for instance if they live in 'small' homes for three or fewer people and have not previously claimed the special rates of Income Support.

Note that people in local authority homes cannot receive Housing Benefit.

HELP WITH THE COUNCIL TAX

In April 1993 the Council Tax replaced the Community Charge (poll tax) as the system of paying towards local government services in England, Scotland and Wales. The rates system continues in Northern Ireland. Under the Council Tax system all domestic dwellings are allocated to one of eight bands (A–H) depending on their estimated value in April 1991. The level of tax for a property in band H will be three times as high as the tax for a property in band A. One bill will be sent to each household. One or more people will be legally responsible for paying the bill although the household can choose how to divide up the bill.

There are various ways that your bill may be reduced and these are summarised below. It may be possible to receive help from more than one of these schemes.

Exemptions Some properties, mainly certain empty ones, will be exempt, which means there will be no Council Tax to pay. For example, your former home will be exempt if it is empty because you are living in a hospital, residential or nursing home, or because you have gone to live with someone else in order to receive or provide personal care.

Disability reduction scheme The property may be placed in a lower band if it has certain features which are important for a disabled person such as extra space for a wheelchair or an additional bathroom or kitchen for the use of the disabled person. If your home qualifies for a reduction your bill will be reduced to the level of tax for the band below the one your home is in. However, this will not be possible if your property is in the lowest band (A).

Discounts The Council Tax assumes there are two or more people living in each property. A discount of a quarter (25 per cent) will be given if someone lives alone and a discount of a half (50 per cent) will normally be given if no one is living there. However, some people will not be counted for the purposes of the Council Tax so discounts may still be given even if there are two or more people in a property. For example, someone who is 'severely mentally impaired' and some carers will not be counted.

Council Tax transitional reduction scheme This scheme will apply in England and Scotland but not in Wales where bills will generally be lower. It will help people who would otherwise face large increases in bills because of the change from the Community Charge to the Council Tax. Any reduction will be given automatically – you will not have to apply. These reductions are not related to your income and savings.

Council Tax Benefit This depends on the income and savings of the person(s) responsible for the bill or the people they live with. It is described in more detail on pages 55–68.

Further information is available from Age Concern England Factsheet 21 *The Council Tax and Older People*, or from Age Concern Scotland.

HELP WITH HEALTH COSTS

Most of the treatment given under the National Health Service (NHS) is free, but there are some things for which most people have to pay part or all of the cost. This section first outlines hearing and chiropody services, which are free under the NHS. It then explains who can get help with the cost of other NHS services such as dental care, eye tests and glasses.

Free NHS services

Hearing aids

You should discuss hearing difficulties with your GP who may, if necessary, refer you to a hospital for tests. If you are prescribed a hearing aid, this will be fitted and issued by a local NHS hearing aid centre. NHS hearing aids are available on free loan; replacements and batteries are also free.

Private hearing aids are usually expensive, but if you do want to buy one, the Hearing Advisory Group at the Royal National Institute for the Deaf will advise about the various kinds available. They can also give advice on other matters concerning deafness. Their address is 105 Gower Street, London WC1E 6AH.

Chiropody

NHS chiropody services are free to everyone, but health authorities vary in the extent of provision. Some are unable to provide a comprehensive service because of a shortage of State Registered Chiropodists and others because of the pressures on financial resources. There may be a delay in being seen or a long wait between appointments. Recognising this, health authorities should give priority to certain groups including older and disabled people.

You may wish to consider private treatment. Not all private chiropodists are State registered, which is the requirement for employment in the NHS. Non-registered chiropodists have various forms of qualifications and training. If you go to a private chiropodist, you should enquire about their training. There are no regulations governing non-registered practitioners. Chiropodists who are State registered can use the letters 'SRCh' after their name; the local NHS chiropody service may keep a list of those registered practitioners who also do private practice.

Help with NHS costs

At the time of writing, the Government is looking at the system of help with NHS costs and changes may be introduced during 1993. To be kept informed of any changes introduced during the year, complete the form on page 129.

If you receive Income Support, you will automatically receive help with the health costs described below by showing your order book or a letter from the Benefits Agency (DSS).

If you are not getting Income Support but have no more than £8,000 savings, you can apply for 'low income entitlement'. If you qualify you will be sent one of two certificates, both of which last for six months. Certificate AG2 entitles you to the same amount of help as people receiving Income Support. If your income is a little higher, you may get certificate AG3, which entitles you to more limited help. To apply for a certificate under the low income scheme, you should get form AG1 from your dentist, optician, hospital or Benefits Agency (social security) office. Remember that if you receive Income Support, you do not need to apply for a certificate.

See Department of Health leaflet AB 11.

Prescriptions

NHS prescriptions are free to women aged 60 or over or men aged 65 or over. However, younger people can also get free prescriptions if they have a low income or suffer from certain 'specified conditions', which are listed in leaflet P 11.

Prescriptions are also free to people receiving Income Support and those who have certificate AG2 on grounds of low income, as described above. People who have certificate AG3 entitling them to partial help with some NHS costs are not able to get help towards the cost of prescription charges.

If you cannot get free prescriptions you may be able to save money by buying a 'season ticket' or prepayment certificate.

See Department of Health leaflet P 11.

Dental care

NHS dental treatment, check-ups and dentures are free if you get Income Support. Treatment will also be free if you have certificate AG2 and the cost may be reduced if you have certificate AG3. Details of how to apply for a certificate are given above. Every time you start a new course of treatment, tell the dentist that you are on Income Support or have a low income.

Unless you are entitled to free treatment or help with the costs, you will have to pay 80 per cent of the cost of most treatment up to a maximum of £250 for one course of treatment.

Since October 1990 there has been a new system of dental care. It is a good idea to make sure that you are registered with a dentist for regular treatment (called 'continuing care'), as this means you will be entitled under the NHS to any treatment that the dentist considers necessary to maintain your oral health.

■ No help is given towards private dental fees. If you want NHS dental care, make sure the dentist is providing you with NHS treatment before you start each course. You can do this when you discuss the proposed treatment with your dentist.

See Age Concern England Factsheet 5 *Dental Care in Retirement* and Department of Health leaflet D 11.

Sight tests and glasses

Opticians may now make a charge for a sight test. Some people are entitled to a free (NHS) sight test. You will qualify for a free (NHS) sight test if you receive Income Support, have certificate AG2 as described above, or belong to a priority group, which includes registered blind and partially sighted people, those who need complex lenses, and diabetics. People who have glaucoma or someone aged 40 or over who is the parent, brother, sister or child of a person with diagnosed glaucoma will also qualify.

Look for an optician who displays a sign that he or she does NHS sight tests because some opticians will only provide private sight tests.

If you have certificate AG3, as explained above, you may get some help towards the cost of a private sight test. If the certificate AG3 says that you can afford to pay less than £12.75 (as at March 1993, although this figure may change in April or during the year), you should ask the optician for form ST(V) on which you can ask for help with the cost of a private sight test. If this test costs more than £12.75, you will have to pay the balance yourself, so it may be worth checking whether another optician might be cheaper.

If you cannot get to the optician's practice for a sight test, you may be able to arrange for an optician to visit you at home. If you are entitled to a free NHS sight test, you will not have to pay for the visit. The cost of a home visit may be reduced if you have certificate AG3.

You are entitled to a voucher towards the cost of glasses provided you get Income Support or have certificate AG2. You may get some help if you have certificate AG3. Do not pay for your glasses if you have applied for help on low income grounds and are waiting for a decision as you will not be able to obtain a refund (unless the glasses were prescribed through the Hospital Eye Service). You will need to wait for your certificate. The voucher carries a financial value linked to your optical prescription; it may cover the full cost of the glasses or be used as part payment for a more expensive pair. If your glasses or contact lenses cost more than any voucher you are given then you will have to pay the difference.

If you need complex lenses, you will be able to receive a voucher from your optician to help pay for the glasses regardless of income and savings. However, the amount of help will be greater if you receive Income Support or qualify on grounds of low income.

Before you have a sight test or get glasses, find out whether you qualify for help. If you will have to pay for some or all of the cost, you may want to check whether another optician might be cheaper, as charges can vary.

See Department of Health leaflet G 11.

Elastic stockings, wigs, fabric supports

Elastic stockings are available on prescription and are free to people aged 60 or over (women) or 65 or over (men). You can also get help with the cost if you have a low income (ie you are on Income Support or have certificate AG2 as described above) but do not qualify on age grounds.

Wigs and fabric supports are supplied through hospitals and are free for in-patients. If you are an out-patient, there are charges depending on the type of wig or fabric support supplied. However, they are free if you are on Income Support or have certificate AG2; if you have certificate AG3 you may get some help with the cost.

See Department of Health leaflet WF 11.

Hospital travel costs

If you get Income Support you will automatically qualify for help with the cost of travelling to and from hospital for NHS treatment. You may also get help towards these costs if you have certificate AG2 or AG3 on grounds of low income. See 'Help with NHS costs' above on how to apply for a certificate. Ask at the hospital for more information.

If you are visiting a close relative in hospital and you are receiving Income Support you may be able to get help with the cost of your fares from the Social Fund (see pp 51–54).

See Department of Health leaflet H 11.

Medical care abroad

You are only covered by the NHS while you are in the United Kingdom. If you are abroad and fall ill, you may have to pay all or part of the cost of any treatment. There are special arrangements with European Community and some other countries which may enable you to get free or cheaper emergency medical care abroad. If you are going to live in another country, you should find out well in advance about your entitlement to medical treatment there.

Before going abroad, get leaflet T4 *Health advice for travellers* from the local post office to find out what cover there might be for treatment in the country you are visiting. It is advisable to take out private medical insurance to cover the full cost of any treatment you may need abroad. Medical treatment is very expensive, as is the cost of bringing a person back to the UK in the event of illness or death.

■ No matter where you are going, check that you have enough travel insurance to cover any emergency expenses you may have to meet.

For further information, write to the Department of Social Security, Overseas Branch, Newcastle Upon Tyne NE98 1YX.

TRAVEL CONCESSIONS

Rail and underground

British Rail give one-third reductions on most types of ticket to people who have a Senior Railcard, which currently costs £16 (March 1993) and is valid for one year. It is available to people aged 60 or over provided proof of age is given. If you have a Senior Railcard, you can also buy a Rail Europe Senior Citizen's Card, which offers discount fares on rail travel in most of Western Europe. Principal stations and travel centres should have the details of how to apply for a Railcard.

If you are severely disabled, you can buy a Disabled Person's Railcard which allows you and a companion to travel at reduced fares. Full details of who qualifies are given in a leaflet available from your local railway station.

Local rail or underground systems not run by British Rail may also offer concessions; you should ask at local offices or stations.

Bus services

In almost all areas of the country, pensioners qualify for some form of concessionary bus fares. Broadly there are four types of scheme:

- travel tokens which can be used for part or full payment of fares;
- flat-rate passes for any length of journey on one bus in a given area;
- half-fare passes, usually limited to off-peak, weekend and public holiday journeys;
- free bus travel passes limited to off-peak, weekend and public holiday journeys.

Apply to your local authority for details.

Taxicard schemes

These are available to disabled people in Greater London, who can obtain an application form from their local authority. At the time of writing under the scheme the passenger pays a flat fare of £1.40 per trip plus any excess over £10.60 on the meter (eg a fare of £13 would cost £1.40 plus £2.40).

Taxicard schemes operate in Greater London with the exception of Barnet, Greenwich, Redbridge and Westminster, which run their own schemes.

Airlines

Some airlines may have concessionary fares for pensioners. Ask at the airline or travel agent for details.

Proof of eligibility

If you are drawing a pension but do not have a pension book (for example, because your pension is paid into a bank account), you can get a card proving that you are a pensioner. Write, quoting your pension number, to the Department of Social Security, Central Pensions Branch, Newcastle Upon Tyne NE98 1YX. If you have no proof of being a pensioner, you may have to produce a copy of your birth certificate or another official document showing your age.

See Age Concern England Factsheet 26 *Travel Information for Older People.*

HELP WITH LEGAL FEES

If you need legal help, you may be able to get this free or at a reduced rate, depending on your circumstances and the type of legal problem you have.

Fixed-fee interview

Some firms offer a fixed-fee interview – up to half an hour of a solicitor's time – for a fee of not more than £5 including VAT. However, it is planned to abolish this system in June 1993 and replace it with a locally based referral scheme. For more information ask your solicitor or an advice agency such as a Citizens Advice Bureau.

ALAS!

If you have had an accident and you want advice about compensation, you can have a free first interview through the Accident Legal Advice Scheme (ALAS!). A local Law Society or a Citizens Advice Bureau will be able to tell you which firms offer this service. They are also listed in the Solicitors' Regional Directory, which can be found in public libraries, town halls and many advice centres, or you can telephone the ALAS! helpline on 071-242 2430.

Legal advice and assistance scheme (Green Form Scheme)

If you are on Income Support or have a low income and have little or no savings, you may get free legal advice and assistance under the Green Form Scheme or you may only have to pay part of your legal costs. A solicitor or Citizens Advice Bureau will be able to tell you whether you qualify for help. If you do, you may get a solicitor's advice, have letters written, have your case prepared for a tribunal (eg a Social Security Appeal Tribunal) or have other legal work done, provided it does not involve going to court or being represented at a tribunal by a solicitor.

However, for most non-criminal (civil) cases in the Magistrates' Court or before a Mental Health Review Tribunal, a solicitor may be able to represent you under the Legal Aid advice and assistance scheme, called 'assistance by way of representation'.

Help with the cost of making a Will through the Green Form Scheme may be available if you are physically or mentally disabled or you are aged 70 or over.

Legal Aid

If you are involved in a civil court case or a case which might lead to court proceedings, get advice from a solicitor, Citizens Advice Bureau or law centre about applying for a Legal Aid certificate. However, civil cases in the Magistrates' Court are usually covered by 'assistance by way of representation', as mentioned above. If you qualify financially and the Legal Aid Board is satisfied that you have a good reason for bringing or defending the case, you will be offered a certificate and will have 28 days to accept or refuse this help. Even with Legal Aid you may have to pay a contribution towards the cost of your case. Legal Aid may not be available for a case involving a small amount of money.

If you gain money or property as a result of winning your case, you may have to pay some or all of your costs to the Law Society, known as 'the statutory charge'.

It is also possible to get Legal Aid for some criminal cases. Check with a solicitor, Citizens Advice Bureau or law centre.

The Government has proposed changes to Legal Aid to take effect from April 1993. These changes are not finalised at the time of going to press so be sure to see a solicitor for advice.

For further information see the *Practical Guide to Legal Aid*, available from the Legal Aid Board, 5th and 6th Floors, 28–37 Red Lion Street, London, WC1R 4PP, Tel: 071-831 4209.

Further Information

This part of Your Rights *gives details about local and national sources of help to contact for assistance and advice. In addition, there is information about ordering DSS social security leaflets, Age Concern England factsheets, and other publications on social security benefits mentioned in the book. Also included is an index to help you find the information you require in the book.*

BENEFITS AGENCY/DEPARTMENT OF SOCIAL SECURITY (DSS)

The Department of Social Security is the Government department responsible for pensions and social security benefits. The levels of payments and the rules for pensions and benefits are set by Parliament but the administration of pensions and benefits is now dealt with by the Benefits Agency, which is described as an 'executive agency of the DSS'.

Sometimes there are two Benefits Agency local offices, one for National Insurance benefits and one for Income Support and the Social Fund. A local library or post office will tell you the address, or look in the telephone book where it will be under 'Benefits Agency' or 'Social Security'. You can contact your local office by telephone, by letter or by calling in. If you have difficulties getting out you can ask for a visiting officer to come and see you.

If you have a problem with the administration of a benefit – for example there is a delay in processing your claim – you can telephone or write to the Customer Service Manager at your local office. Social security leaflet BAL 1 *Have your say* tells you how to make comments on the service you receive. If you are still dissatisfied then get in touch with a local advice agency or your MP.

National Benefits Agency/DSS addresses

Central Pensions Branch/
Overseas Branch
Newcastle Upon Tyne
NE98 1YX
Tel: 091-213 5000

Attendance Allowance Unit
Norcross
Blackpool
FY5 3TA
0253 856123

Social Security Freeline

For general advice and information on all benefits telephone:

0800 666 555 (English)   0800 289 188 (Urdu)

0800 521 360 (Punjabi)   0800 252 451 (Chinese)

0800 289 011 (Welsh)

9.30am–4.30pm weekdays

For information about benefits in Northern Ireland telephone:

0800 616 757

9.30am–4.30pm weekdays

Benefits Enquiry Line

For advice and information about disability benefits and form completion service telephone:

0800 882 200

9.00am–4.40pm weekdays

SOURCES OF LOCAL HELP

Age Concern (Old People's Welfare)

Most areas have an Age Concern or Old People's Welfare group which provides services and advice. You can find the address from the phone book, library or Citizens Advice Bureau, or you can write to the appropriate national Age Concern (addresses on page 127) for the address of your nearest group.

Citizens Advice Bureau (CAB)

The local offices provide advice and information on all kinds of subjects including social security benefits, housing and consumer problems. You can find out where your nearest CAB is from the phone book or at your local library.

Law centre

There may be a law centre giving free legal advice in your area. Check in the telephone book or at a Citizens Advice Bureau, or look at the Legal Aid Solicitors list in the library.

Local authority/council

In England and Wales the structure of local government depends on whether you live in a county, or a metropolitan or London borough. The situation in Scotland and Northern Ireland is different and not covered here. In England and Wales if you live in a county the district council will deal with Housing Benefit, Council Tax Benefit and other matters to do with the Council Tax. You will need to contact the county council about social services. In a metropolitan or London borough there will be just one authority that will deal with the Council Tax, Housing Benefit and social services. Some authorities have welfare rights workers to advise on benefits. You will find the address of your council in the telephone book under the name of your county, metropolitan or London borough, or ask at your local library.

Local councillor

A councillor for your area may be able to help with problems with the local authority. You can get the names of the councillors for your 'ward' from the town hall, library or Citizens Advice Bureau.

Local Government Ombudsman

If you feel you have suffered because of maladministration in the way the local authority has dealt with your case, you can make a complaint to the Local Government Ombudsman. You can do this directly or through your local councillor. Ask a local advice agency or councillor for further information.

Member of Parliament (MP)

Your MP may be able to help with problems involving Government departments. If you do not know who your MP is, ask at the town hall, library or Citizens Advice Bureau. Most MPs hold regular surgeries locally; or you can write to him or her at the House of Commons, London SW1A 0AA.

For a complaint about unfair treatment by a Government department (eg a delay with a claim for a social security benefit), ask the MP to refer your complaint to the Parliamentary Ombudsman.

Trade union

If you were a member of a trade union before retirement, it may be worth contacting your local branch, particularly for problems over a pension from work.

Welfare rights and money advice centres

There may be an independent welfare rights or money advice centre locally. Money advice centres generally deal with debt problems and may only accept referrals from other agencies.

SOURCES OF NATIONAL HELP

The national organisations listed below may be able to help or put you in touch with a source of advice.

Carers National Association
29 Chilworth Mews
London W2 3RG
Tel: 071-724 7776

Child Poverty Action Group
1–5 Bath Street
London EC1V 9PY
Tel: 071-253 3406

Counsel and Care
Twyman House
16 Bonny Street
London NW1 9PG
Tel: 071-485 1566

Disability Alliance
1st Floor East
Universal House
88–94 Wentworth Street
London E1 7SA
Tel: 071-247 8776

Energy Action Grants Agency
PO Box 1NG
Newcastle Upon Tyne
Tel: 0800 181 667

Occupational Pensions Advisory Service
11 Belgrave Road
London SW1V 1RB
Tel: 071-233 8080

Royal National Institute for the Blind
224 Great Portland Street
London W1N 6AA
Tel: 071-388 1266

Royal National Institute for the Deaf
105 Gower Street
London WC1E 6AH
Tel: 071-387 8033
071-388 6038 (Qwerty)
071-383 3154 (Minicom)

For information about national organisations in Scotland, Wales and Northern Ireland contact the appropriate national Age Concern (addresses on p 127).

FURTHER READING

Factsheets from Age Concern England

Age Concern England produces factsheets on a variety of subjects, some of which have been mentioned in *Your Rights*. Single copies are available free. To receive any of these or a complete list of factsheets send an sae (9" x 6") to Age Concern England, 1268 London Road, London SW16 4ER.

Benefits Agency/DSS leaflets

As well as the leaflets mentioned in *Your Rights,* there is a catalogue of all the social security leaflets produced (Cat 1). Social security leaflets should be available from your local Benefits Agency (social security) office, and they are sometimes in libraries, post offices or Citizens Advice Bureaux. Alternatively you can write to the following address, stating which leaflets you need: DSS Leaflets Unit, PO Box 21, Stanmore HA7 1AY.

Department of Health leaflets are available from Health Publications Unit, Heywood Stores, Manchester Road, Heywood, Lancashire OL10 2PZ.

Other publications

For detailed information on services and benefits for disabled people, you may wish to get the *Disability Rights Handbook,* £7.95 (£5 for individuals receiving means-tested benefits), available from the Disability Alliance, 1st Floor East, Universal House, 88–94 Wentworth Street, London E1 7SA.

For detailed information on all social security benefits, with reference to the relevant Government legislation, you may wish to refer to the *National Welfare Benefits Handbook* (income-related benefits), £6.95 (£2.65 for individual claimants), and the *Rights Guide to Non-Means-Tested Social Security Benefits*, £6.50 (£2.45 for individual claimants). Both books can be ordered from the Child Poverty Action Group, 1–5 Bath Street, London EC1V 9PY. They may also be available for reference at your local library.

ABOUT AGE CONCERN

Your Rights is one of a wide range of publications produced by Age Concern England – the National Council on Ageing. In addition, Age Concern England is actively engaged in training, information provision, research and campaigning for retired people and those who work with them. It is a registered charity dependent on public support for the continuation of its work.

Age Concern England links closely with Age Concern centres in Scotland, Wales and Northern Ireland to form a network of over 1,400 independent local UK groups. These groups, with the invaluable help of an estimated 250,000 volunteers, aim to improve the quality of life for older people and develop services appropriate to local needs and resources. These include advice and information, day care, visiting services, transport schemes, clubs and specialist facilities for physically and mentally frail older people.

Age Concern England
1268 London Road
London SW16 4ER
Tel: 081-679 8000

Age Concern Scotland
54A Fountainbridge
Edinburgh EH3 9PT
Tel: 031-228 5656

Age Concern Wales
4th Floor
1 Cathedral Road
Cardiff CF1 9SD
Tel: 0222 371566

Age Concern Northern Ireland
3 Lower Crescent
Belfast BT7 1NR
Tel: 0232 245729

KEEPING UP TO DATE

Your Rights is based on the information available at the beginning of March 1993 and the benefit levels will normally apply until the first week in April 1994. A new edition of the book will be published next year to cover the period from April 1994 to April 1995. However, sometimes changes are made during the course of a year.

If you would like us to inform you of any major changes introduced before April 1994, please cut off this page and return it to the address below.

Dear Age Concern
Please send me details about any major changes
introduced before 1994

NAME (BLOCK LETTERS)

SIGNATURE

ADDRESS

POSTCODE

Publishing Department
Age Concern England
1268 London Road
London SW16 4ER

PUBLICATIONS FROM ◆◆◆BOOKS

A wide range of titles is published by Age Concern England under the ACE Books imprint.

Money Matters

Earning Money in Retirement
Kenneth Lysons
Many people, for a variety of reasons, wish to continue in some form of paid employment beyond the normal retirement age. This helpful guide explores the practical implications of such a choice and highlights some of the opportunities available.

£5.95   0–86242–103–9

Your Taxes and Savings
Sally West and Jennie Hawthorne
Explains how the tax system affects people over retirement age, including how to avoid paying more tax than necessary. The information about savings covers the wide range of investment opportunities now available.

Further information on application.

Using Your Home as Capital
Cecil Hinton
This best-selling book for home-owners, which is updated annually, gives a detailed explanation of how to capitalise on the value of your home and obtain a regular additional income.

Further information on application.

General

An Active Retirement
Nancy Tuft
Full of information on hobbies, sports, educational opportunities and voluntary work, this practical guide is ideal for retired people seeking new ways to fill their time but uncertain where to start.

£7.95   0–86242–119–5

Eating Well on a Budget
Sara Lewis
Completely revised, the new edition of this successful title offers sound advice on shopping and cooking cost-effectively and includes wholesome original recipes for four complete weekly menus.
£5.95   0–86242–120–9

Living, Loving and Ageing: Sexual and personal relationships in later life
Wendy Greengross and Sally Greengross
Sexuality is often regarded as the preserve of the younger generation. At last, here is a book for older people and those who work with them which tackles the issues in a straightforward fashion, avoiding preconceptions and bias.
£4.95   0–86242–070–9

Health and Care

The Community Care Handbook
Barbara Meredith
The provision of care in the community is changing as a result of recent legislation. Written by one of the country's foremost experts, this book explains in practical terms why the reforms were necessary, what they are, how they will work and who they will affect.
£11.95   0–86242–121–7

Your Health in Retirement
Dr J A Muir Gray and Pat Blair
This book is a comprehensive source of information to help readers look after themselves and work towards better health. Produced in an accessible A–Z style, full details are given of people and useful organisations from which advice and assistance can be sought.
£4.50   0–86242–082–2

Housing

Housing Options for Older People
David Bookbinder
A review of housing options is part of growing older. All the possibilities and their practical implications are carefully considered in this comprehensive guide.

£4.95   0–86242–108–X

An Owner's Guide: Your Home in Retirement
Co-published with the NHTPC
This definitive guide considers all aspects of home maintenance of concern to retired people and those preparing for retirement, providing advice on heating, insulation and adaptations.

£2.50   0–86242–095–4

If you would like to order any of these titles, please write to the address below, enclosing a cheque or money order for the appropriate amount. Credit card orders may be made on 081-679 8000.

Age Concern England (DEPT YR3)
PO Box 9
London SW16 4EX

INDEX